Worldviews
Crosscultural Explorations of Human Beliefs

second edition

Ninian Smart

Prentice Hall, Englewood Cliffs, New Jersey 07632

Library of Congress Cataloging-in-Publication Data

Smart, Ninian (date)
   Worldviews: crosscultural explorations of human
beliefs/Ninian Smart--2nd ed.
     p.   cm.
    Includes bibliographical references (pp. 168-170) and
index.
    ISBN 0-02-412031-6
    1. Religions. 2. Ideology. I. Title.
BL80.2.S62   1995
291--dc20   94-28525
                                    CIP

Editorial/production supervision
  and interior design: **Joan E. Foley**
Acquisitions editor: **Ted Bolen**
Editorial assistant: **Meg McGuane**
Copy editor: **Henry Pels**
Cover designer: **Anthony Gemmellaro**
Cover art: **Craig Aurness/Westlight** (face);
    M. Angelo/Westlight (background)
Buyer: **Lynn Pearlman**

© 1995 by Prentice-Hall, Inc.
A Simon & Schuster Company
Englewood Cliffs, New Jersey 07632

Printed in the United States of America

10 9 8 7 6 5 4 3 2 1

ISBN 0-02-412031-6

Prentice-Hall International (UK) Limited, *London*
Prentice-Hall of Australia Pty. Limited, *Sydney*
Prentice-Hall Canada Inc., *Toronto*
Prentice-Hall Hispanoamericana, S.A., *Mexico*
Prentice-Hall of India Private Limited, *New Delhi*
Prentice-Hall of Japan, Inc., *Tokyo*
Simon & Schuster Asia Pte. Ltd., *Singapore*
Editora Prentice-Hall do Brasil, Ltda., *Rio de Janeiro*

To Marilis

UNIVERSITY OF
WOLVERHAMPTON
KNOWLEDGE • INNOVATION • ENTERPRISE

Harrison Learning Centre
City Campus
University of Wolverhampton
St Peter's Square
Wolverhampton
WV1 1RH
Telephone: 0845 408 1631
Online renewals: www.wlv.ac.uk/lib/myaccount

Telephone Renewals: 01902 321333 or 0845 408 1631
Online Renewals: www.wlv.ac.uk/lib/myaccount
Please return this item on or before the last date shown above.
Fines will be charged if items are returned late.
See tariff of fines displayed at the Counter.

Contents

Preface

I hope that this book will be a good introduction to the modern study of religion. To examine human beliefs and the feelings and practices that accompany them, we need to go beyond traditional religions, even though much of this second edition is about how we might understand them better. Therefore, I have given the book a broad scope to cover both religious and secular worldviews (such as nationalism, humanism, and Marxism). In brief I pay attention to all the major forces of belief and feeling that animate our world.

Worldviews: Crosscultural Explorations of Human Beliefs is for students of all ages and explorers of all walks of life. I hope it may be a steppingstone to richer knowledge and clearer understanding. Mostly it is about knowing other people; such knowledge is at the heart of humanistic education and the social sciences.

I owe a lot to students and colleagues in Lancaster, England, and in Santa Barbara, California. I have benefited especially from teaching large classes of usually eager students in California, for most of whom the study of religions and the analysis of worldviews is new. I learned much from this experience, but I have also learned from the many good discussions I have had with M.A. students, especially in Lancaster, often fresh from their own experiences in various countries and occupations.

Since the first edition was published, momentous events have occurred: The Soviet Union collapsed and new nations have come into existence, from Kazakhstan to Estonia. The old communist empire in Eastern Europe has broken up. Even in China, new market forces have replaced the older system. Scarcely any Marxist states still carry on—North Korea and Cuba rather feebly. So the major alternative ideology to democratic capitalism has given up its materialistic ghost. Revelations since the collapse of Marxism seem to confirm that it did preside over an evil empire; not that there are not evils elsewhere, but nowhere as deep as those of the cynical and inefficient Soviet system. A major reason for this second edition is that some of my previous examples and illustrations no longer apply.

In a way these recent world events confirm the importance of what I say and imply in this book. The worldview aspect of human existence is confirmed in its crucial role. The Soviets collapsed in part because few continued to believe in the system. Practical Marxism was perceived as fruitless. Without some democratic controls it had become a tyranny that did not work. But there are also lessons for other ideologies and religious. When Italy has the lowest birthrate in the world, and still is largely Catholic under a pope preaching against artificial means of contraception, you can see that bourgeoisie is the greatest contraceptive of all, and older systems of authority are breaking down. For this reason if for no other we are still living in a new religious age. Conservative backlashes against individualism are fine, but they only shout louder against the decay of authority. The secret of all this is that people chose the bible and the pope. They may receive grace, but they are not chosen. It is by their continuing loyalty that they confer their authority on their leader and their sources.

I am grateful to the publishers for reissuing this book. I originally wrote it one summer in my wife's lovely Tremezzo on Lake Como, Italy. She is my great facilitator and, of course, my favorite companion. I had as much pleasure realigning the book's arguments for this second edition as I did writing the first editon. Though the book is written for the general public, I believe it contains vital truths that all students of history and human affairs would do well to heed.

Santa Barbara, California   Ninian Smart

Introduction

We know more about each other today than we have ever known before. Among the branches of learning and science that have formed this knowledge, the study of religion has a central place. As an educational experience it provides fine training for our world. The reason is simple: Human beings do things for the most part because it pays them to do so, or because they fear to do otherwise, or because they believe in doing them. The modern study of religion is about the last of these motives—the systems of belief that, through symbols and actions, mobilize the feelings and wills of human beings. In addition to examining traditional faiths, the modern study of religion also looks at secular symbols and ideologies—at nationalism, Marxism, democracy—which often rival religion and yet in an important sense are themselves religious. Thus, the modern study of religion helps to illuminate worldviews, both traditional and secular, which are such an engine of social and moral continuity and change; and therefore it explores beliefs and feelings, and tries to understand what exists inside the heads of people. What people believe is an important aspect of reality whether or not what they believe is true.

The English language does not have a term to refer to both traditional religions and ideologies; the best expression is perhaps "worldviews". In this book I shall use "worldviews" in a general sense to refer to both religion and ideologies and also to refer specifically to secular ideologies.

With electrons or moons or eggs or chestnut trees there is no need to understand what they think. Science does not have to worry about any conscious insides that such things might have. They can be treated just as physical objects (although as it turns out they are composed mainly of space). But with human beings things are otherwise. Why did Caesar cross the Rubicon? What were the roots of the Iranian Revolution? Why did the Holocaust occur? Why is Richard happy? The answers to such questions must make some reference to what people feel, the ideas they have, the structures of belief of their society—in a word, to human consciousness. The study of religions and secular worldviews—what I have termed "worldview analysis"—tries to depict the history and nature of the beliefs and symbols that form a deep part of the structure of human consciousness and society.

This modern study of religion is not much more than a century old, although its roots lie in the last decades of the eighteenth century and the period known as the European Enlightenment. For most of human history, people have had rather rudimentary ideas about their own and other people's beliefs. Often imprisoned within a culture or a credo, they have not had the desire or the chance to venture on a more detached and sensitive exploration of religion. Too much tied up with their own concerns, they have often found it easier to dismiss the faiths and feelings of others as heretical, devilish, ignorant, or antisocial, and this has been so especially in the West. Yet paradoxically, the modern study of religion started in the West, and through comparative research, historical inquiry, and a broadening of sympathies this study has opened up the entire sweep of religious experience. The study has gone far beyond its Western origins. Important work on religions is being done in India, China, Japan, Africa, and elsewhere. The modern study of religion is becoming global. This is natural. Our contemporary world is now bound together tightly. We live in the age of the global city.

The most compelling pictures in our times are those magical photographs of the Earth taken from halfway to the moon: The shining blue ball bandaged lightly in its atmospheric wool; the dim shapes of great continents showing darkly through the gaps. Ours is no longer the wide, wide world of older days, nor is Earth any more just a fertile, soil-clad floor out of which life emerges, as our ancestors might have pictured it The images of the Earth we now have tell us that we live together on a little ball, bound together, and to it, in a web of air and food. And the very cleverness that took men so far in space to take those photographs also allows us to send a missile to our enemies in half an hour, or to fly for fun to the farthest continent in hardly more than a day. If, that is, we have the money for missiles and fun: Most people do not.

The fact that human civilization is now so tightly knit that its every crisis sends ripples around the globe, is one reason why the modern study of religion, with its emphasis on understanding rather than preaching, is so important. Even if we do not agree with one another it is vital that we should at least understand one another. We have a long way to go in achieving this understanding, however; the importance of the modern study of religion has not, on the whole, penetrated fully to people's consciousnesses—whether in academic life, in government, in the media, or in business.

There are two reasons why this is so: One has to do with older conceptions of what it means to study religion; and the other has to do with the compartments into which knowledge is carved. The heart of the modern study of religion is the analysis and comparison of worldviews; from this broader point of view, the problems caused by the older images of religion and by the compartmentalization of religious studies can readily be seen. But before coming to that let me say a word about what I mean by "the modern study of religion."

The modern study of religion takes religion as an aspect of life and tries to understand it historically and crossculturally. It applies the insights of various disciplines—such as psychology, anthropology, sociology, and linguistics—to illuminate its dynamics. It is parallel to, and sometimes overlaps with, political science and economics.We are all to some degree or other political animals, because power is a fact of life; and we are all economic beings, for financial exchange is a fact of life. But we are all also religious beings, for orientation to life is itself a fact of life; and we are all in one way or another so oriented. We are not, of course, necessarily religious in any formal or traditional sense. Many people are agnostics, atheists, nonobservers of customary tradition. But whether we have spelled it out to ourselves or not, each one of us has a worldview that forms a background to the lives we lead. The modern study of religion has as one main focus the exploration of such worldviews, particularly the more widely held belief-systems and especially those of a traditional kind, such as varieties of Christianity or Buddhism.

A Native American proverb says, "Never judge a man til you have walked a mile in his moccasins." Much of what the modern study of religion involves is such moccasin-walking. It is a kind of voyage into other people's and our own living hearts, a travel into the sentiments and ideas that animate people, often at the deepest level. It means also travel into the past, swimming upstream along the river of time, trying to reach the mind of Paul or Buddhaghosa or Confucius. It is in itself a noble and imaginative task, to find out what the world looks like from another person's or society's point of view. It is difficult, though, and that is one reason why I shall spell out some of the ways it can be made easier.

The modern study of religion is not perceived by most people very clearly as yet, because they usually and not surprisingly identify the study of religion with traditional patterns—learning catechisms; going to seminary; studying the texts of the faith; or training to be a minister, a priest, a rabbi, or other religious leader. Such traditional confessional (as we may call it) study continues and is necessary if traditions are to maintain themselves. But it is not the same as the modern study I have described. It does not pretend to be crosscultural. Its main concerns are with the truth of one's own faith, not with the understanding of other worldviews. It starts from the assumptions of faith. It does not need to be dispassionate.

People thus often think of the religious expert—Billy Graham, Pope John Paul II, the Dalai Lama, a seminary professor, a learned rabbi—as a spokesperson for a particular faith. And that is fine if what is wanted is an expression of faith or opinion starting from the particular tradition to which the spokesperson belongs. But such persons are part of the traditions for which they speak: They are part of what the modern student of religion seeks to understand. They are themselves part of the data. Thus, while the Pope is the authority for Catholics, others may know more about religions, including Christianity, then he does. For example, it is my job, as a religious scholar, to understand religion; it is his, as a religious leader, to *be* religion.

If older conceptions of religious study as preparation for preaching get in the way of people's understanding the significance of the modern study of religion, so does the compartmentalization of knowledge. Thus, a student goes to one department to study Christianity, typically, but to another department to study Marxism; to study the social meaning of Judaism she goes to one department, but to another department to study the social meaning of Australian aboriginal religion; to study modern existentialism she goes to one department, but to another department to study Zen. The study of worldviews is not only crosscultural but also crossdisciplinary; it occurs in the contexts of religion, political science, sociology, anthropology, philosophy, Oriental studies, and others.

If a visitor from another world were to come down and hover invisibly over our planet, he would see religions and ideologies in conflict, and he would see people moved by symbols both modern and traditional. Would such a visitor so easily distinguish the Olympic stadium from the temple, or the hammer and sickle from the Islamic crescent, or the psychiatrist from the priest? Would he carve up the world the way we do in the modern West? Such a visitor, reporting back home to some far galaxy, might say, "These humans have all kinds of orientations to the world, and all kinds of symbols, and all kinds of ways of training their minds and feelings. Some they call religions, when there is some kind of looking upward to a heavenly sky or inward into the depths of their being. Mostly these ways of thinking and acting have had a very long history (by their standards), up to two or three thousand years."

And if that is what a dispassionate observer would say, does it not call into question our compartments? The modern study of religion is beginning—rightly—to look toward breaking these down and analyzing all worldviews and human symbols together, whether they are traditional or not.

Thus, a main part of the modern study of religion may be called "worldview analysis"—the attempt to describe and understand human worldviews, especially those that have had widespread influence—ranging from varieties of Christianity and Buddhism to the more politically oriented systems of Islam and Marxism, and from ancient religions and philosophies such as Platonism and Confucianism to modern new religions in Africa and America. To see how they work we must relate ideas to symbols and to practices, so that worldview analysis is not merely a matter of listing beliefs. A Christian's belief in Christ is a matter of experiencing him and partaking of him in the communion service; a Buddhist's belief in the impermanence of things is a matter of seeing this impermanence revealed through meditation; the Marxist's belief in the labor theory of value is a matter of readiness to act against what she perceives as exploitation. In a word, belief, consciousness, and practice are bound together.

An educated person should know about and have a feel for many things, but perhaps the most important is to have an understanding of some of the chief worldviews that have shaped and are now shaping human culture and action. It is for this purpose that I try to present some of the main elements and themes of the modern study of religion here.

But beyond knowing the geography of human consciousness, I may wish to explore my own orientations, to try to articulate my own beliefs, to reflect about life and the world: to form or clarify the basis of my own worldview. Such a goal goes beyond the comparative study of worldviews; it is itself a quest. This also can form a living part of the modern study of religion, for once we have traveled into other minds and times we may want to return to our own lives. What do these symbols mean to me? Toward which orientation should I set my own soul's face?

Here the student of worldview analysis becomes the self-explorer, the quester. As we shall see, there can be a fruitful interaction between quest and analysis. But the modern study of religion is initially less involved in judgment than description. And that itself is an exciting but difficult task. And if, as we have suggested, we should not judge a person until we have walked a mile in his or her moccasins, then we must embark first upon the description of religions and religion. However, that in turn requires us to reflect about ways and means, about methods and lines of approach.

In Chapter 1, I shall give a more detailed map of the study of religion and worldviews. In Chapter 2, so that we may bear in mind the general character of worldviews, I shall present an inventory of all the the major faiths and belief-systems found both in today's world and in the past. In Chapters 3 through 8, I shall discuss some of the theories and themes arising out of various disciplines used in the study of religion. These six chapters correspond to the six dimensions of religion, to which I shall come in a moment. In Chapter 9, I shall consider what is happening at the developing stage of human belief and practice, and on into the future. In the postscript, I consider what the individual can do to continue his or her exploration of worldview analysis or to carry his or her own quest further.

The model of six dimensions of religion (which I first described in *The Religious Experience*, Chapter 1, and later amplified in *The World's Religions* and elsewhere) is useful for giving a rounded and realistic picture of a religion. Often histories of religions tend to concentrate too much on the doctrinal or the organizational aspects, especially in the case of Christianity, which in many ways is the least well-described religion in the standard histories. You can find books on Christianity with almost nothing written on worship and other ritual aspects. Who would dream of writing a book on Buddhism as a religion without including quite a lot on the subject of meditation and other practical features of the faith? The six dimensions are:

Doctrinal or philosophical

Mythic or narrative

Ethical or legal

Ritual or practical

Experiential or emotional

Social or institutional

These dimensions are not listed in order of importance, which may vary depending upon the religion or denomination in question. Doctrines are much more vital among Catholics than among Unitarians; and philosophical ideas are more central among Buddhists than among Jews. Ritual is central to traditional Confucianism but not among Quakers. And so on. But some elements of each dimension are found in most or all religions and among secular worldviews. Their delineation, therefore, creates a realistic picture (or maybe I should say sculpture, to give a sense of roundedness) of a religion in action.

1. Doctrinal. A religion typically has a system of doctrines. Christianity holds that the world depends on God, that God is Three in One—namely, Father, Son, and Holy Spirit—that Christ is both God and man, and so on. These are part of the doctrinal dimension of Christianity. They tell Christians about the nature of God and his relationship to the created world and the human race.

2. Mythic. Typically a religion has a story or stories to tell. But they are not just any old stories—they are ones that quiver with special or sacred meaning. In the field of religion such stories are called myths. The word does not imply, as it does in everyday speech, that such stories are not true, just "myths", but often "myth" is used technically to refer to stories of the gods or other significant beings who have access to an invisible world beyond ours. Thus, the mythic dimension of Christianity focuses on the story of the Fall, when the first man and woman alienated themselves from God and were driven from their earthly paradise; the subsequent contracts between God and the people of Israel as part of his plan to save the human race from its state of alienation; the coming of

Christ and his death and resurrection; the beginning of the Church, which carries forward the work of salvation; and the promise that Christ will come again to earth to wind up human history in a great climax of judgment and bliss.

   3. Ethical.   A religion has an ethical dimension. Believers are enjoined to observe certain rules and precepts. Thus, in Christianity Jesus commanded his followers to love one another and to love their enemies. There are also the commandments derived from the Old Testament that forbid killing, adultery, stealing, and so forth.

   These three dimensions—the doctrinal, mythical, and ethical—form a web of belief, but the beliefs are truly understood only in the context of experience and practice. So in Christianity, doctrines about God are not just about some neutral and remote being who created the universe; God is a being who is actively worshiped. Christians pray to him, and he brings his influence to bear upon a person's inner life (such influence being referred to usually as "grace"). The story of his dealings with humanity implies that somehow the Christian can identify with the story by taking part in certain acts and practices. For instance, in the Lord's Supper or Mass, the Christian is involved in a replay of the last events of Jesus' life, and absorbs his life-giving power through partaking of the bread and the wine, which present afresh the body and blood of the Savior. Thus myth is often conjoined to ritual acts that replay them and so convey their meaning to believers in a concrete way.

   4. Ritual.   So, typically a religion has a ritual dimension. Christianity, for example, usually involves its followers in acts of worship, praying, singing hymns, hearing the appointed passages from the Bible, and such sacraments (rituals through which God's grace is conveyed) as baptism and communion (the Lord's Supper, Eucharist, Mass, Liturgy—different branches of Christianity use different words).

   5. Experiential.   Ritual helps to express feelings—awe and wonder, for instance—and can itself provide a context of dramatic experience, when the believer feels immediately and strikingly the presence of God. In Christianity, there is often emphasis on the experience of conversion, or being "born again"; while the monastic tradition (especially important in Catholic and Eastern Orthodox Christianity) is often the means of nurturing the experience of inner illumination in which the mystic feels a kind of union with Christ. Such experiences are part of the *experiential* dimension of religion.

6. Social. Any tradition needs some kind of organization in order to perpetuate itself. It thus embeds itself in society. In Christianity the churches provide a strong *social* dimension.

For reasons of continuity in the overall argument, I shall, in the various chapters mentioned above, deal with the dimensions in a different order than listed here. I'll first discuss the experiential dimension, since experience has played and still plays such a central part in the history of religion. Consider Paul's conversion on the Damascus road and the experiences of the risen Christ among the other apostles; consider the light that lit up the Buddha's mind under the Bo Tree; consider the tremendous, even painful experiences of Muhammad while receiving revelations from Allah; look to the lives of mystics and prophets and others in a variety of faiths. All these testify to the way experiences can dynamize religion and so dynamize the world. Thus a whole Islamic civilization had its roots in Muhammad's experiences, a whole Buddhist civilization in the Buddha's enlightenment, a whole Christian civilization in the experiences of the Hebrew Prophets and of the early Church. There were many other factors indeed, but the experiential dimension had an explosive and creative part to play. So in Chapter 3 we will explore the varieties of religious experience and problems about their power and meaning.

In Chapter 4 we will see how myth works and how it remains in secular form a powerful ingredient in today's world, as human beings search for new identities and find them partly in the story of their past. In Chapter 5 we shall see how religious doctrines are formed, in interaction with myth and experience, and how they relate to other areas of human knowledge such as modern science. In Chapter 6 we will learn how moral values themselves reflect the understanding of the world found in vision, story, and doctrine, and how far we can see a universal ethic among the great traditions. In Chapter 7 we turn to the ritual dimension, and the way symbols are used, while in Chapter 8 we shall see how religion operates socially.

In these explorations there will be a chance to see how the modern study of religion can throw light on theories of the individual and of society. For we are able to look upon such theories from a crosscultural perspective: Does Freud's account of religion work for Buddhism? Can the Marxist analysis of religion successfully explain the varieties of religious forms and the persistence of religion in the modern world? What is the relation between religion and the rise of capitalism? To what extent do theories of religion depend upon an estimate of the truth of religion? Many questions flow from the writings of some of the great thinkers of modern times— Sigmund Freud, Karl Marx, Rudolf Bultmann, Mircea Eliade, Max Weber, Carl Gustav Jung, Ludwig Wittgenstein. We may only touch upon these figures and themes, but at least we shall have opened up perspectives on a strange and enchanting landscape, beckoning us forward to further thoughts about the enigmas of our existence and the forces that drive human processes onward.

It may seem strange that it is possible to illuminate so much of modern life and theory by beginning from the study of traditional religions. Many people think that religion, for all its spurts of resurgence here and there, is on the way out—destined in the end to wind up as fairy tales. But it happens that symbols often work most powerfully when they are unseen and unrecognized. The historian of religion is sensitive to the way symbols help to shape our existence, and is therefore able to perceive them more easily in our daily world. This is a perception he or she shares with the depth psychologist. Thus, if we hear it said that "modern people" no longer need religion, we need to see what a loaded notion *modernity* is. (Now some academics like to say that we no longer need religion in a postmodern age—that too has its symbolic load.) Doesn't it carry with it some kind of myth? Isn't there the suggestion that we have entered a new era in which science and technology will help to solve our problems, leaving behind the superstitions of the past? Doesn't it dress itself in lasers and rockets and glittering machines? Doesn't its fantasy life flow in science fiction? Doesn't it, in its myth of history, suggest the superiority of those nations and cultures that can devise the best machines and systems of management? Such a notion as *modernity* has much of the force and power of older religious symbols, but the apostles of secular modernity would not thank me for saying so. They have made a judgment about religion, a negative one. In fact, by drawing a line between the secular and the sacred they have already made a value judgment (secular is modern and good, religion is old and bad). So they feel that calling the cult of modernity a kind of religious attitude, as I have just done above, undermines and challenges the very distinction that helps to give them a sense of superiority. Nevertheless, it may be illuminating for us to see how the symbol of modernity works, and in this the historian of religion will have some insights to share. Thus it is that the modern study of religion (and note, by the way, how I too am implicitly calling on the values of modernity) starts from the old in order to throw light upon the new.

But in speaking of the modern study of religion we should not attempt to create a closed compartment. It is convenient to think of worldview analysis as a field of study, but it must by necessity overlap many other disciplines and approaches. Already in my list of famous names I have hinted that it overlaps depth psychology (Freud and Jung), sociology (Weber), economic history (Marx), early Christian history (Bultmann), the comparative study of religion (Eliade), and philosophy (Wittgenstein). But equally we could look to literature—you can learn much about worldviews through Shakespeare and Dostoyevsky and Steinbeck; or to art history—you can learn much through Giotto and Indian sculpture; or to music. The symbolic life of human beings ranges across the humanities and the social sciences. The modern study of religion presents a perspective on the whole of human life.

So let us then accept the invitation to enter our world and see it with new and yet old eyes.

Chapter

1

Exploring Religion and Analyzing Worldviews

What I have called the modern study of religion has evolved from a number of dramatic shifts in thinking and knowledge occurring mainly in the last century.

Developments in the Nineteenth Century

The nineteenth century saw the vast spread of Western colonial conquest. It brought Europe into ever closer ties with the peoples of the East and the Southern Hemisphere. This was a great spur to scholarship in Asian and other languages. These languages helped unlock the religious treasures of Islam, of India, of Buddhism, of the Chinese tradition, and of Africa. People in the West could begin to think about the place of Christianity, and for that matter Judaism, among the great religions of the world. Already the material for the comparative study of religion was being accumulated.

The nineteenth century also saw the publication of Darwin's controversial theory of evolution. This new way of thinking about the origin of the human race challenged earlier Western beliefs about the way humankind was created by God. It called into question the literal truth of Genesis. But more, it suggested that not only had the human race evolved, gradually and over a long period of time, but that socially and in other ways it was still evolving. There were a number of new theories suggesting ways in which religion itself had evolved. Such theories were backed up by data collected by the new science of anthropology, the study of small-scale societies. By supposing that the cultural development of (say) Australian aborigines corresponded to a similar stage of development in an earlier phase of human evolution, anthropologists thought they could chart the history of human development in general—and, in this case, the history of religion.

Anthropologists hypothesized that humans graduated from animism (belief in living powers dwelling in material and natural objects), to polytheism (belief in many personalized gods), to monotheism (belief in one God), and maybe beyond, to atheism. Most of these theories are now no longer thought to be valid, partly because they often reflect the assumption of Western culture that it has achieved the highest stage of development and achievement—a possibly arrogant value judgment rather than a scientific diagnosis. Still, ideas of cultural evolution greatly influenced speculations about patterns of similarity among the myths, symbols, and rituals of widely distant societies.

The theory of evolution also, as it happened, combined with a whole series of developments in history, archaeology, and language study, throwing new light upon the ancient Middle East and on the early stages of Jewish and Christian history. The new approaches suggested it was possible to treat the Bible not so much as a sacred, infallible scripture, but rather as a collection of historical documents for the scholar to probe. To some degree this brought a challenge to Christian orthodoxy, and even now there are debates about the literal truth of the Bible. But this shift in attitude was a stimulus to look at the scriptures of all nations and traditions more dispassionately. And this gave further impetus to the formation of what one scholar, Max Müller, called "the science of religion," and what others have referred to as the history of religions.

Another school of nineteenth-century religious thought helped to breed new psychological and social theories. It was the notion that God is a projection; that is, he is like a picture thrown on a screen who seems real to us and existing "out there," but nevertheless really has his source in human feelings or human culture. This idea was taken up by Karl Marx, who saw traditional religion as a side effect of the economic relations within feudal and capitalist societies. Human beings, unable to master earthly economic and social problems, project their desires upon the universe. There is a heaven awaiting the oppressed, while at the same time the ruling classes use the divine authority figure to serve their interests and keep workers and peasants in subjection. Later a different theory of projection was formulated by Sigmund Freud, only the emphasis was more on the dynamics of the nuclear family and the child's developing feelings about his father and mother, rather than on society as a whole. God is an enormous Father. Such projection theories were a stimulus to social and psychological explorations of religion.

But these theories were themselves open to criticism; for didn't they presuppose a view about the world, a view in which God is an illusion, and material forces can explain human development? And isn't Marxism itself possibly a sort of projection, offering the illusion of a material paradise in the human future, rather than a heaven in the sky? Doesn't Freudianism itself become a sort of religion, with psychoanalyst as priest? Why shouldn't the view that religion is our illusion itself be an illusion?

Whatever theory we may end up with about religion, and whatever comparisons we may wish to make about religions, we first face the problem of describing religions and secular worldviews as they actually are. And this is where modern scholars of religion have looked for a way of "moccasin-walking" that begins not with claims of religious truth or cultural superiority, but tries to treat religions and secular worldviews on their own terms. It is a way that respects the standpoint of the believer.

Such an approach is sometimes called the *phenomenological* method, following the German philosopher Edmund Husserl (1859–1938). Husserl tried to describe experience as it actually is, without the distortions created by prior beliefs and assumptions. Phenomenology asks that we step back and look afresh at our own feelings, perceptions, and the whole flow of consciousness. Can we see a rose afresh without thinking of all the associations the word "rose" suggests? Phenomenology is a little like the method of some contemplatives engaged in religious meditation (in the Buddhist tradition, for instance). But for our purposes Husserl's philosophy need not detain us, for the word "phenomenology" (the study of what appears) has been used in a less technical way by historians of religion. What they borrow from Husserl is the idea that the believer's world can be described without introducing the assumptions and slant of the investigator. For various reasons I think it is best not to use the word "phenomenology," but rather the phrase "structured empathy."

Empathy literally means "feeling in"; it is getting at the feel of what is inside another person or group of persons. It is not quite the same as sympathy, "feeling with" (*pathy sym* rather than *pathy em*), for sympathy means I *agree* with the other. Even if I do not agree with the other person, however, I can still have empathy. For instance, we might feel what it is like to have been a Nazi revering Hitler without in any way sympathizing with her, or with Hitler's aims. Feeling what her worldview is like would help us to understand why Hitler was as successful as he was. But even more important, empathy helps us to better grasp the facts—for the facts include the way she feels and thinks about the world.

This is why, too, the empathy needs to be *structured*. We have to comprehend the structure of another's world; and in general, we have to try to understand the structures of belief inside the head of the believer. So what is it like to be a Buddhist in Sri Lanka or a Catholic in Ireland? We need to know quite a lot about Buddhist ideas and practices as found in Sri Lanka, and quite a lot about Roman Catholic beliefs and practices as found in Ireland.

I shall return to all this, for there is much more to be said. But for now let us agree that the neutral, dispassionate study of different religions and secular systems—a process I have called worldview analysis—has been an important ideal in the comparative study of religion. It emerged in the nineteenth century as a way of treating the world's religions on their own terms.

For we must remember that, in the past, most of the Western study of religion has been thought of as Christian theology—the study of the texts, history, and doctrines of the faith on the assumption that Christian faith, being true, was superior to all others. When other religions were studied, they were usually compared—unfavorably—to Christianity. They were studied, for instance, as background for Christian missionary work in Africa, Asia, and elsewhere. At worst they were regarded as examples of religious idolatry, and at best as incomplete pointers to the higher truth to be found in Christ. Hinduism, for example, was a religion in which, as the nineteenth-century Anglican bishop Heber wrote in a famous hymn: "The heathen in his blindness/ Bows down to wood and stone." Either that, or else it was regarded as a religion whose noblest aspects needed completion by Christ, who is, to quote the title of a book by a famous Scottish missionary to India, J. N. Farquhar, *The Crown of Hinduism.* But historians of religion engaged in worldview analysis see things more dispassionately. The inferiority or superiority of Hinduism is, in their view, a matter of judgment, bias, evaluation, or belief; but it is neither relevant nor helpful in describing what Hinduism is, what it feels like, what its many faces are.

The worldview analyst has struggles on two fronts. To the right are those "traditional" believers (Christian and otherwise—but since we are speaking chiefly of Western scholarship, it is mainly traditional Christians and Jews we have to consider) who regard a more dispassionate and nonjudgmental description of the world's beliefs as an implicit threat to the faith. To the left are those humanists and Marxists who think that religion is irrational and so has to be explained away as some kind of projection. Both groups forget that religions are what they are and have the power they have regardless of what we may think about their value, truth, or rationality. They also forget that in a plural world, questions of the truth of any one religion over any other are debatable—and so we have to listen to one another.

The "Comparative" Study of Religion

For a long time, and especially in Europe, a strange division arose between religious scholars who belonged largely to Christian faculties of theology or divinity schools, and scholars engaged in the comparative study of religion. It was as though all religions other than Christianity (and, by implication, Judaism because it belonged to the same tradition of "revealed" religion) were to be treated as a separate group. It was sometimes argued that Christianity is unique and cannot seriously be compared to other religions. Only in the 1960s did the English-speaking world, and to some degree northern Europe, arrive at a broader and more integrated conception of the study of religion in which various religions and worldviews, Christianity included, are dealt with together. Thus, the modern study of religion, emerged partly out of the comparative study of religion and looks at Christianity, too, as a "world religion"—not as the exclusive concern of Christian scholars.

But I should add that many of the best historians of religion have been Christians. Although there have been problems among those Christian theologians who think that comparative religion makes people comparatively religious (to echo a famous and disdainful quip by the Roman Catholic writer Ronald Knox), many Christians have had a more encouraging view of the modern study of religion. (Actually, as far as my experience goes, Knox is quite wrong.)

So far, in sketching some of the threads woven into the fabric of religious studies, I have used, interchangeably, the phrases "history of religions" and "comparative study of religion." Both phrases have somewhat confusingly been in vogue.

People have used "the comparative study of religion" because, as a famous slogan has it, "If you know one, you know none." This means that knowledge of one religion can throw light upon another, and knowledge of another upon one's own, or that of one's own culture. For instance, in a number of traditions water is a symbol of chaos, and so even of death. Knowing this helps to illuminate the ritual of total immersion practiced by many Christians at baptism. The devotee dies to the world and then rises again out of the waters of chaos and death with the risen Christ. Another example is this: Some Christian mystics say that it is impossible to refer to God with words, for in the higher stages of the path of meditation all words and images disappear. It turns out that similar things are said in Buddhism and in the Hindu tradition. So this similarity of expression suggests that there may be here some kind of universal human experience, and that the comparative study of religion helps bring this universality to light.

Moreover, if I cross the frontiers of my own culture and travel into the minds and hearts of another tradition, I am bound to make some kinds of comparisons, even if only in realizing that I must not read the assumptions of my own background into the lives of other people. If I as a Christian explore the meaning of the Sabbath for a Jew, I must become aware of deep differences in attitude, despite the use of a common word, namely "Sabbath." In order to understand the Buddhism of Sri Lanka or Thailand I must put behind me the thought that the supreme focus of faith is God, for the Buddhism of Sri Lanka does not focus on a Creator and has quite a different picture of the universe from that found in Genesis. I must not start from the assumptions of baseball in trying to understand cricket. Exploring another tradition should bring contrasts, not just similarities, to the surface; and this is what making comparisons means. So, in an important sense, every time I cross the mental frontiers of my tradition and society I am engaged in a comparative study. And indeed, comparative study is possible within traditions and societies, as well as outside them. I am an Episcopalian, and the adjustments I need to make in order to understand what it is like to be a Southern Baptist or a Mormon or a New England Catholic are already considerable. I must not assume that I know my neighbor. And even if for some purposes it is useful to talk about Christianity or Buddhism, it is in fact more realistic to speak of Christianities and Buddhisms. Each has more than fifty-seven varieties. In brief, then, the whole enterprise of crosscultural understanding is comparative.

It also happens that modern scholars of religion have done much work on themes and types, looking at similar phenomena across the board. I have mentioned mysticism—here trying to see if there is a single shining core of inner experience to be found among those in different religions who engage in meditation. Another example is this: There are recurring patterns in different stories of creation and in myths of catastrophe, such as the story of the Flood. Or, we can see how there are types of religious leadership in both East and West—there are monks and nuns, priests, prophets, and other ecstatic visionaries. Or again, the notion of religious sacrifice seems to be a widespread religious phenomenon. All these observations are to do with *types* of religious phenomena.

Somewhat confusingly, a number of well-known writers (such as Gerardus van der Leeuw, the Dutch scholar; Geo Widengren, the Swede; and Mariasusai Dhavamony, the Indian) have used the term "phenomenology of religion" when referring to their comparative studies of religious themes and types. We thus have another meaning for that lengthy word "phenomenology." I think it is clearer if we refer to this particular kind of study as "typology" or "thematic comparison," or perhaps even "morphology," the cataloging of forms.

But although it is true that there is a comparative element in the study of religion, the phrase "comparative study of religion" is rather awkward and has in any case become dated. It sometimes had negative connotations; as we have seen, in the old days it could be a conscious or unconscious means of expressing Western superiority when other faiths were compared to their detriment. Partly because of the influence of the modern Chicago school of religion, led by Mircea Eliade, and partly because the International Association for the History of Religions uses the term, it is more common now to talk of "the history of religions." This covers both the writing of the history of individual faiths as well as thematic reflections about contrasts and comparisons.

Some like also to use the word "crosscultural" to express the fact that we have to see the world religions together. The term has great merit in that it suggests that the traffic is not all from one culture to others, but can cross in differing cultural directions, East and West and North and South. The message here is that we should not be busy merely imposing Western themes and categories on non-Western faiths, but that we should also be using Eastern and other categories to throw light on Western religion. Thus, for example, a major element in the Hindu tradition is the fervent worship of a personal God, thought of as Vishnu, or Krishna, or Shiva, or the divine female Kali. (About the last, an anecdote is told: A Hindu swami, or religious teacher, was once pressed to tell on television what God is really like; he surprised his American white male interviewer by saying "She is black.") Anyway, such devotion—or faith— called *bhakti* is an important strand both in Hinduism and in later Buddhism. It is reasonable, vis-à-vis Christianity, to say that many Protestant hymns and Paul's theology also express a variety of *bhakti*. There are many other non-Western categories that could be used across the board with profit. We could begin to ask questions like "What is distinctive about Christian *bhakti*?" So the modern study of religion can also be looked on as crosscultural.

This makes sense; we do, after all, live on the same globe. We are now moving into a period of global civilization in which we begin to share one another's ancestors and achievements. Beethoven is played in Tokyo and Indian music in New York, and the citizen of the world can draw on the ancestral wisdom of both Socrates and Confucius and the art of Paris and Nigeria. So too can the modern study of religion become genuinely crosscultural and therefore global.

These comparative themes become especially important when we begin to test wide-ranging theories about religion. For instance, the great sociologist Max Weber (1864–1920) hypothesized that Protestantism was a main factor in the rise of capitalism in the West. To test his theory, he looked at how things fared outside Europe, in the Islamic, Indian, and Chinese worlds. For if we say that certain religious factors A and B give rise to result C in one culture, then we need to discover whether A and B are present in other cultures that do *not* manifest C. Either they are not present, or at least, not jointly; or, if they are present, then we should look for some further factor D to tell us why A and B gave rise to C in one culture but not in the others. We cannot put human societies and human histories into a laboratory, but we can use global history as a kind of laboratory. This is where the social sciences can make use of crosscultural comparison. Weber was a major crosscultural pioneer in the fields of religion and economics. He described religious attitudes that, in his view, greatly influenced the rise of capitalism. The Protestant faith, according to Weber, placed great emphasis on inner-worldly asceticism, in which the faithful lived actively, but austerely, *in* the world (rather than living the more contemplative life of the monastery, which other faiths emphasize). In particular, Weber identified the influence of Protestant reformer John Calvin, whose teachings, coupled with his establishment of a religiously controlled state in Geneva, were important. These factors motivated the middle classes to work hard and spend moderately, and were thus central to the rise of capitalism. What, by the way, do we say about the Buddhist and Confucian values lying deep in the social structures of Japan? How far have they been the source of Japan's great technological and economic miracle?

The fact that the modern study of religion is crosscultural helps to strengthen the belief that we should include secular world-views within its scope. For although it may seem to us in the West that the division between secular and sacred is "natural," and that political ideologies such as Marxism belong to a different category from religions, other, non-Western perspectives may not necessarily divide human realities the same way. Thus, if we look to China, we find that Maoism comes as a direct alternative to the old tradition of Confucius, which likewise contained a philosophy of how to run society. They both play in the same league.

We can sum up what has been said or implied about the modern study of religion as follows:

First, it is plural, dealing with the many religions and secular worldviews of the globe.

Second, it is open-ended in the sense that it includes consideration of belief-systems and symbols lying beyond the frontiers of traditional religions.

Third, It treats worldviews both historically and systematically, and attempts to enter, through structured empathy, into the viewpoint of the believers.

Fourth, it makes thematic comparisons that help to illuminate the separate traditions.

Fifth, it is polymethodic: It uses many methods drawn from various disciplines—history, art history, philology, archaeology, sociology, anthropology, philosophy, and so on.

Sixth, it aims to show the power of religious ideas and practices and their interactions with other aspects of human existence.

Seventh, it can set the scene not only for an educated understanding of the world and its various belief-systems, but also for a personal quest for spiritual truth.

A central part is played in all this by the process of structured empathy. It is the way we cross our own horizons into the worlds of other people.

Exploring Italian Catholicism

Let us see what structures are involved in trying to understand a particular form of Christianity. Suppose we are trying to understand the nature and shape of Roman Catholicism in Italy.

First, we have to reckon that it is part of the family of faiths known as Christianity, and some general picture needs to be gained of the main teachings and practices of the religion. It is useful here to use the six dimensions as an inventory, and we have already seen something of the general structure of Christianity from our discussion of these.

But second, particular features of Roman Catholicism need to be understood. There is, for instance, the fact that it is *Roman.* Think of the many strands of meaning and association the word "Rome" trails with it. Rome is the eternal city, the hub of the old Empire, still lively in the consciousness of the Italian. It remains a center of pilgrimage. Incidentally, pilgrimage is an important religious theme in the great traditions—consider Banaras in India beside the holy Ganges River; Mecca, the annual meeting point of millions of Muslims; Jerusalem, whither many a medieval traveler went with great peril and hardship, and where Jews and Christians still flock eagerly today. Think of Compostela in Spain, and Guadalupe in Mexico. The idea that one should travel to the "center" of one's cosmos, the spiritual hub of the universe, is an old one.

The centrality of Rome goes with the centrality of the Pope, successor of Peter—who was martyred in Rome perhaps on the very spot where St. Peter's now stands—and of Paul, the great apostle who ended his days in the imperial capital. Thus Rome is an ingredient in the continuance of the Christian myth, stretching back through the Resurrection and the life of Christ to the Jewish hinterland of the faith. It stretches forward through the life of the Church, which has a divine essence, was founded by Christ, is animated by the Holy Spirit, is led by Peter's successors, and is the earthly vehicle for the transmission of the divine teachings and the life-giving rituals of Christianity.

This mythic dimension of Roman Catholicism, then, is the story or the set of stories that give the faithful a sense of identity and belonging to a divinely instituted organization. The central element in their experience of the Church is the heart of its ritual dimension, namely the Mass. We cannot truly understand the power and meaning of Roman Catholicism without having a sense of the Mass.

This raises some questions of method. How can I have that sense without in some way participating in the Mass? I can of course rely somewhat on films and literary works that may present the Mass, which may be a vital help in the search for empathy. It would be better to attend at least one or two Masses as a sort of participant. In the field of anthropology, living with the people one is trying to understand is commonly called "participant observation." It is a way of doing fieldwork. In religion fieldwork is also important. Even if it is not always feasible for the explorer of religion to do it, it is something that he or she should bear in mind, for there will be many opportunities in life for travel and for explorations. And if a person remains truly interested in understanding his or her fellow human beings, then these opportunities can provide ways of deepening knowledge.

If one is trying to enter into the minds of those who attend Mass (I am here assuming that the person seeking to do so is not Roman Catholic), one has to suspend one's own beliefs. It is not the point to say, "These practices are based upon a set of doctrines that I do not share." It is vital,by contrast, to think what it would be like to believe those things. One's own biases and commitments fall away. This suspension of one's own assumptions is sometimes referred to (following Husserl) as *epochē (pronounced* ep-och-ay, with *och* rhyming with "loch", *ay* rhyming with "day"). Another word that is used is "bracketing," for one "brackets out" one's own beliefs for the time being.

This may seem difficult, but the difficulty depends partly on the person. A religious fanatic, for instance, may find it impossible to practice such bracketing. Certain kinds of religious commitment may stand in the way of understanding. Sometimes firm atheists, too, find it hard to enter into the spirit of religion. But generally, I think it is not too hard for people to have enough awareness of themselves to be able to draw a line between their own beliefs and feelings, and those of others.

The Mass as a ritual needs quite a lot of explanation. The participant observer can often do with a running commentary. The observer has to see it as the central way in which the faithful perceive themselves as having access to the power of Christ. He or she has to understand how the bread and the wine not only symbolize but actually (from the point of view of the faithful) *contain* the substance of Christ himself. He or she has to see how, for the Catholic, the central religious "specialist" is the priest. It is not the preacher, for instance, although preaching is one of the priest's functions; nor is it the monk, although in fact monks are part of the fabric of

Catholicism and often have priestly functions. He or she must understand that the rite of the Mass is central to Catholic Christianity, and it is the priest who is authorized to conduct the rite. He is the one who can bring into being again and again this great encounter between Christ and the faithful. So the participant observer must try to see the Mass not only through the feelings of the faithful but also through their complex beliefs—beliefs that relate to, among other things, the institutions and nature of the Church.

Traditionally, a bell is rung at the moment during the Mass when the bread and wine are consecrated—when, that is, they cease being ordinary articles of food and drink and become the sacred substance of God himself. Sometimes the bells of the campanile or church tower are also rung, tolling solemnly. This solemn moment has its own feeling. It is *numinous*, to use a word coined by Rudolf Otto (whose work will be discussed in Chapter 3): It contains mystery and inspires awe. The faithful bow in silence before the solemn event. The observer, too, has to have a sense of this solemnity, this numinous feeling.

This is one place where religion tends to differ from secular worldviews. The latter do not have such a vital concern with this sense of the Other, this feeling of divine presence, this perception of unseen Power. But even so there are parallels to traditional religion. In Moscow, tourists—who are, in effect, pilgrims—lined up daily to look at the embalmed body of the great Lenin, chief founder of the Revolution, and so of the new world in which they lived. Such magical figures as the Beatles have had similar effects of strange power upon their fans; the death of John Lennon had many of the overtones of a solemn religious event, for he summed up in his person, for the "believers," a set of values—peace, love, the music of gentle protest. In the heyday of the Cultural Revolution in China the reverence for the power of Mao's thought and person reached religious proportions.

With the sense of the power of Christ in the sacrament, the pious Catholic also believes that Christ's goodness and holiness are such that the person who takes communion—that is, receives into him- or herself the substance of Christ—must be in the right state. He or she must not be in a state of sin, which is a kind of impurity and at the same time an alienation from, a being cut off from, God. So it is that the Church has the institution of confession where the faithful unburden themselves of their sins and receive forgiveness from God through the priest. Their sins are no longer dogging them, and they are now in a renewed state of purity. Then they can with a good conscience receive Christ.

In this way and in others the ritual and experiential dimensions of Catholicism link up with ethics. Italians, it is true, often disregard the moral and social teachings of the Church. Like many other Catholics, they do not always follow it in matters related to divorce and abortion. But in general the Church is seen as the authority on morals, and so the person's daily life is integrated into religion.

Another way to get a feel for Roman Catholic values is through its symbols. The crucifix, showing the suffering Christ upon the Cross (often in realistic and bloody detail), tells the ordinary person that God can identify with his sufferings and the sufferings of his neighbors. Another crucial symbol is the Virgin Mary. How can we understand the Roman Catholic tradition, and Italian Catholicism in particular, without seeing the vibrant importance of the cult of the Blessed Virgin Mary? The story of Jesus' mother is given further definition by the Church—for instance, in the claim that she was taken bodily up into heaven at the time of her death. The Virgin is the representation, so important for Italians, of ideal womanhood and ideal motherhood. Mother and yet virgin, she is also inspiration for the priest who is a Father and yet is celibate.

The statues of the Virgin and the crucifixes of the suffering Christ are among the ways in which material things are used in the course of worship. The statues are more, and other than, art: They give a sense of the living presence of Christ and the saints. They are, in effect, acts of worship congealed into stone and plaster and metal. Much can be learned about religion from the way it expresses itself through such sculptures, paintings, and other objects. Also, as it happens, quite a lot can be learned from their absence. Many Protestant chapels and meeting houses are empty of any decoration or statues. Such artifacts are thought of as challenging the biblical command not to make graven (that is, sculptured) images. They are thought to encourage idolatry—idolatry being the worship of that which is not God. Similarly, Islam forbids the use of images of any kind. But the Roman Catholic tradition and the Eastern Orthodox wing of Christianity have, in their own ways, made use of visible representations of Christ, the Virgin, and the saints.

Both of these traditions venerate the saints. Here the observer needs to understand that although the Italian may call on St. Anthony, or San Pellegrino, or the Virgin Mary for help, he does not mean to worship them as gods: He or she calls on them because they, being close to God in heaven, can serve as helpers in petitioning God.

These, then, are some of the ways in which the observer begins to penetrate into the full meaning and context of the Mass. He or she thus begins to understand what it is like to be an Italian Catholic.

The ordinary Italian, even if a pious Catholic, includes more in his or her total worldview than the Catholic faith, it is true. There are, for instance, beliefs and values connected with the nation of Italy; and Christian faith has to be thought of in relation to other kinds of knowledge, such as that provided by science. So the whole comes to constitute a loosely put-together patchwork. But for certain purposes we can see it as a version of the Catholic faith, which blends religious and secular values. The believer thinks of the faith as relating to the ultimate sense of the world, and thinks of God as the creator and guide—not just of the Church, but of the nation and the material cosmos as well, and of science as well as faith.

In such ways the observer builds up a picture of what it is like to be an Italian Catholic, ranging through the dimensions of the faith and so mapping its structures, and trying to get the feel of the believer's attitudes toward the various focuses of his or her religion—the Trinity, the Madonna, the Pope, and the local priest.

Exploring the Past and the Present

In conducting this exploration we are taking a slice in time: We are getting the feel of what the faith is like in the twentieth century. We could have tried to find what the faith was like in the fourth century, after the conversion of the emperor Constantine; or in the thirteenth century, at the time of the great saint and philosopher St. Thomas Aquinas; or in the sixteenth century, during the upheavals of the Protestant Reformation; or in the nineteenth century, during the fight for Italian independence and unity. Here we would be looking at other slices in time. Each slice represents a synchronic, or "same-time" picture.

It is not, of course, easy to find out what the faith was like in times gone by. Historical records are sometimes inadequate, and the nature of daily life often was not recorded since much of it would have been taken for granted and not referred to in documents. We cannot get into a time machine and glide back to Acquino in southern Italy to interview the young Aquinas, or speed silently back to the days after Constantine's legions were victorious at the Battle of the Milvian Bridge under the proud banner of Christ, or even make the shorter trip to see the world during the life

of Verdi, when his operas thrilled all Italy and his name was a rally-
ing cry for Italians against their oppressors.

Still, the past is not wholly hidden from us. The historian of
religion looks to see how the present structures of religion have
emerged from the deep and complex web of interactions of humans
and events in times gone by. The historian can also, by seeing
something of the religious heart of a tradition—the numinous experience, the piety of saints, the force of religious ideas, the lure of rituals, the dynamism of myth, the strength of the institutions of the
faith—,estimate how far religion has molded society and how far
society by contrast has shaped religion. Usually it is a complex two-
way interaction. Anyway, the historian can present not just a series
of synchronic slices but also something of a moving picture. The
historian deals with a "through-time," or *diachronic*, picture.

Methods of Exploration

The synchronic of "same-time," indeed contemporary, analysis
through structured empathy of a particular faith in a given context
is more or less the same as the methods of analysis used in anthropology. It is true that the social anthropologist tends to deal with
small-scale cultures, often in the Third World, and it is also true
that he or she will probably be interested in much else besides religion and worldviews—for example, the way kinship works; for the
webs of family and clan life vary greatly among differing people and
give different perspectives on a number of other things in their societies. But there is much that the worldview analyst can learn from
anthropologists; the study of religion and anthropology are closely
bound together. The same applies to sociology. The latter is deeply
involved in the structures, including the belief-structures, of modern industrial societies. A joke has it that anthropology is about
them and sociology is about *us*. But together, sociology and anthropology cover all cultures, and although their emphasis is on the
social dimension of cultures (the way people act in and through the
webs of social relations they are involved in), they nevertheless can
throw much light on religion, too. Thus, the sub-disciplines of
anthropology of religion and sociology of religion have come into
being. Religion has its own social dimension; thus, we can ask the
same question about today that the historian may have asked
about the past: How do religious beliefs, feelings, values, experiences, rituals, and institutions interact with society as a whole, and
the ideas and feelings other than those associated with a given religious tradition? To take a case from today: How does religion affect

the media in the United States, and conversely, how do the media help to influence and shape religion? Is the television preacher the shaper of the system, the victim of the system, or both? Such questions are of profound interest for various reasons. To name but one: if religion still has a powerful function in society, we can infer something about religion's future.

If the explorer of religion needs to know something of the history of religions, it follows that he or she must come in contact with those people who, in one way or another, serve the historian in his probings: the archaeologist, who turns up old statues of the Buddha, or Dead Sea Scrolls, or ancient temples, or the models of soldiers buried in China's distant past; the language specialist, who has managed to decipher ancient languages and who supplies the key to understanding old scriptures; the art historian, who can trace developments in the way religion was understood visually; and so on.

The explorer of religion can learn much, too, from literature. Thus the novelists of modern times have often managed much more successfully than historians to create living pictures of religion in action. In his famous book *A Passage to India*, the English writer E. M. Forster (1879–1970) portrayed the subtle clashes between differing worldviews—Hindu, Muslim, Christian, Indian, British—in India under British rule in the early years of this century. In *The Brothers Karamazov* the great Russian writer Dostoyevsky (1821–1881) depicted in a most dramatic way some of the values and problems of Russian Christianity in the second half of the nineteenth century. In *Darkness at Noon* Arthur Koestler (1905–1988) gives an inside view of Marxist faith and its disintegration. Here and elsewhere there is a whole range of what may be called "worldview analysis in fictional form." The fact that it is fiction is one main reason why it goes beyond history. The historian has to write about what he or she can know. Sometimes in writing a biography—say, of Gandhi or of John XXIII—a historian can flesh out a living figure. But for the most part the records are too sketchy to be able to give that full flow of a person's inner life which the novelist and the dramatist try to portray. They weave that flow from their own imaginations. Theirs is a creative structured empathy: They project their characters on a screen and then see how they move and feel. They are both inside and outside their characters.

Of course, we cannot rely solely on fiction. Fiction has to be complemented by the realities of actual testimony and actual records. Religious writing often concerns the individual person, or at least the lone practitioner. We can see this in the guides to the art of meditation that have been written in differing religious traditions; and in the autobiographical poetry and prose of some of the great figures of the traditions, such as the monks and nuns of the *Elder's Verses* in Buddhism; and in the accounts by the Catholic mystic St. Teresa of Avila (1515–1582) of her inner life. Are there universal themes to be found in religious experience and feeling? This is one of the starting points for modern studies, most notably pioneered in *The Varieties of Religious Experience* by the American philosopher and psychologist William James (1842–1910). From his work and that of others, and from the speculations of Sigmund Freud (1856–1939), C. G. Jung (1875–1961), and other depth psychologists, the field known as the psychology of religion has arisen. Recent evidence suggests that religious experiences of quite a dramatic kind are much more widespread and varied than had previously been thought. What are we to make of them? Are they hints of heaven? Are they illusions?

We can begin to see why we refer to the modern study of religion as polymethodic—using the methods and ideas of many overlapping disciplines. This is not surprising, for the human being has varied relationships, and cannot be reduced to a single dimension of existence. Thus religion, pervading life in a strong or weak manner, has to be seen in many relationships. It has to be seen in relation to the past, so we need history to understand it; it needs to be seen socially, so we need sociology; it needs to be seen in relation to individual development, so we need psychology; it needs to be placed in religious context, so we need worldview analysis; it needs to be seen in relation to human consciousness, so we need literature and other ways into the feelings of others. And as a combination of all these things, it needs structured empathy.

There is a story of a man who felt ill, but in a vague way. He worried so much that a friend insisted on taking him to a clinic, where he saw all kinds of specialists: heart, lung, eye, brain, and so on. Each of them pronounced him healthy. At the end he said he still felt ill. "But," said his friend, "none of these specialists has found anything wrong with you." "But they haven't looked at *me*," the man said. Likewise it is important that even though we use many approaches to religion, we do not forget that in the end, religion is people.

Exploring Symbolic Themes

Each person is unique; but even so, people think and feel according to patterns. The modern study of religion, in describing the forms that religion and symbolism express, gives shape to the language of life—the language of images and actions. If we can understand the themes that recur throughout religions, then we can more clearly decipher the meaning of life around us. This is where the typology of religion, as I have called it, is important. From another perspective we can call it the exploration of symbolic themes.

We have some such themes woven into the fabric of Italian Catholicism; in the Mass, for instance. The Mass is a sacred meal, although it is reduced to brief essentials as far as the actual eating and drinking go. But it does present to us anew the Last Supper when Jesus was with his close associates and friends. It should lead us to see something of the symbolic meaning of eating together. Consider how we often celebrate events through a banquet—a special meal expressing the togetherness of the group usually relating to some cause or some association—a school reunion, a political party, a retirement dinner, a wedding, and so on. We may be led to ask whom we share food with: What people would we and what people would we not ask to our homes to share a meal? This question can lead to a consideration of matters of purity in food. Why do some religious traditions reject certain kinds of food? Even the most secular person in Western society rejects certain foods—dogmeat, for instance (though some other cultures eat dogmeat readily), and horsemeat (though in parts of Europe it is considered a delicacy). Is it that we feel that dogs and horses are too close to us because as pets and in sports they enter into semi-personal relations with us? Once we begin to think about the meaning of food and drink we are given a marvelous opportunity to think again about what is, after all, so close to us that we fail to notice it; our whole way of living and acting is drenched in meanings.

Or consider the symbolism of cities. In religion there is the quest for the City of Zion; and indeed, in the last book of the New Testament, Revelation, heaven is depicted as a marvelous, jewel-spangled city. The destination of pilgrimage is often a city, for the holy city is seen somehow as being at the center. Here (in the center) is one of the great elementary symbols of human life. Jerusalem is at the center of the world, for the Christian, because it was the scene of the climax of the drama of Jesus' life. In the modern world the state capital is usually seen as the "center." It is from there that power radiates. Nations sometimes build new capitals to symbolize a fresh beginning, casting off old associations as the nation restores itself; thus Pakistan built its new capital Islamabad (City of Islam) partly to cast off the associations of the conquered past. The British built New Delhi (based on Old Delhi) to show off the new empire replacing the old Mughal Empire it had conquered. Australia, once it was freed from all but the most formal ties with the mother country (and consider the symbolism contained in ideas like "mother country" and "fatherland"), built its new federal capital in a stretch of bush at Canberra. A century and a half earlier the United States celebrated its status by creating a capital at Washington. These all are relatively new centers; but often it is the ancient centers that have the greatest magnetism—Banaras, Rome, Mecca, Athens, Istanbul.

But there is something about the traditional West European city that holds our attention. Coming toward Canterbury or Salisbury or Cologne from afar one sees at its heart, and rising above it, a great cathedral. The Gothic spire points to heaven: Its whole message is one of straining upward. Inside, its pillars soar. They do not just bear a load. They are not squat. They yearn upward. So the cathedral is a stone act of prayer, of aspiration, of adoration. The traditional Western city had, at its heart, the symbolism of heaven. But nowadays, buildings in modern cities often climb higher. In New York, St. Patrick's Cathedral is dwarfed by the glittering rising columns of skyscrapers: buildings scraping heaven, now not so much pointing to heaven as symbolizing the height humans can attain. Wealth and dynamism here have their architectural language, and they dwarf the pointing fingers of St. Patrick's. Again, New York, like many other cities of the New World, is laid out in a grid; somehow this speaks to us of the rational mind, the conquest and control of the land. It foreshadows the rectangular landscapes of the American Midwest. The old European city tends to be more chaotic, with lines running hither and thither in bursts of design, such as the Mall in London (appropriately running from the Admiralty to the Palace, from one Britannia to another). Manhattan has its crookedness in Broadway: perhaps here there is a feeling for the arts and drama, which do not run along the right angles of the rational mind.

Once we look around us we find that our life is drenched in meanings, and everything has its symbolic sense, often changing, differing in one culture and time from others. The crosscultural exploration of religious and symbolic themes is a way we can understand this world of meanings. With worldview analysis comes symbolic analysis, for ideas need symbols to gain a grip on the world, and so stimulate action. It is no coincidence that between doctrine and ethical practice lies myth; for the stories which give us identity and a sense of direction also contain a strong infusion of symbolic elements. Thus Christ's sacrifice is like the breaking of bread; and just as in a family meal I commune with my fellow human beings, in the sacred meal I gain solidarity with the sufferings and glory of Christ.

We can see that an essential ingredient of the modern study of religion is *symbolic analysis*, which tries to throw light on the various themes that can be discovered crossculturally through the exploration of various worldviews. It is important that the universal and the particular be combined. Thus, the figure of Christ on the cross is an instance of a more universal or general theme, the suffering hero; but it also has a very particular meaning in relation to the unique characteristics of Jesus' life, death, and resurrection.

Crosscultural exploration through symbolic analysis tries to make the strange familiar and the familiar strange. On the one hand, crosscultural exploration gives us a more familiar idea of what it is to be a Muslim in Iran or a Buddhist in Thailand. On the other hand, we begin to look afresh at many of the things we took for granted in our own lives and religious traditions. See them afresh and the familiar things seem strange.

This strangeness also leads us to ask questions anew. Not so long ago, I finished a course I had given on Christianity, in which I tried to describe it as one might any other faith, coolly but with structured empathy (or so I hoped). A student of mine said he had, as a result of the course, become a Christian. Previously, he had been so put off by preaching and slanted presentation that he had not realized that Christianity seen afresh was much more interesting and, for him, more compelling than he had ever imagined. In other words, he had been led to ask new questions. By contrast, those who have never questioned the values and beliefs they were brought up with may, through the realization of the plural richness of human religions, come to ask questions about their faith. So, although I have up to now stressed the descriptive and "bracketed" approach to worldviews, there is no doubt that sooner or later questions of truth arise. What is the truth of religion?

Theology and the Philosophy of Religion

If these questions of truth arise from within the context of religious belief, they sometimes get worked out in terms of what in the West is called *theology*. Strictly speaking, the word ought to have an adjective in front of it—Christian, Jewish, Catholic, Protestant, Reform, Orthodox, and so on. For theology implies acceptance in broad terms of the truth of the tradition in which one is working. A

Christian theologian accepts the Christian faith. This is the context in which many great Western theologians—Augustine, Aquinas, Luther, Karl Barth, to name but a handful—have worked. They have tried to present the religion of their tradition in a new way, in response to changes in the wider world. Thus, the modern Christian theologian has to see the doctrine that God created the universe in light of modern discoveries about the vast size of the cosmos and the long history of the planet Earth. How does he look on Genesis and its story of creation? The theologian has to see what the meaning of Christian love is in the context of a shifting modern society. How does he look upon divorce or welfare? In all sorts of ways the theologian is interpreting the Bible and the tradition so that the meaning of the message is given an expression that makes sense today. In other words, Christian theology is a response from within the tradition to questions that arc put to it by the changing world of knowledge and action.

But not all those who think about religion are committed to a particular faith. There are more general questions about the truth of religion that arise across the frontiers of any given faith. They are questions that crop up for anyone who takes religion and truth seriously. Usually such questions are thought of as "philosophical," and it has become common to think of philosophical thinking about religion as "the philosophy of religion."

The philosopher of religion asks questions about the validity of religious experiences. Do they tell us about the nature of life and the world around us, or are they just subjective feelings? If I feel vividly that I am one with nature and that all things in this wonderful universe are interconnected, does such a flash of insight really have any validity,or is it just me reacting, perhaps for some purely physical reasons—like taking a drug? Or are drugs, too, windows on reality?

Is there any good reason to believe that there is a God? People say that they have had experience of God; what does this actually mean? Although we think that the universe must have had some sort of beginning, does this mean that we have to suppose that there was a Creator who got it going? And when did He (or She) begin? And if He or She could be without a beginning, why shouldn't the universe also be beginningless?

Given that there are so many different faiths and ideologies in the world, how can we tell which is the truth? Are they all true up to a point? And if so, is one truer than the others? And how do we tell?

These thoughts are at first bewildering, and we seem to flounder. But they are questions that, in one way or another, each of us has to respond to, for we do in a sense live our lives according to the conclusions we reach. If I really think that religious experience has no validity, then there isn't much use bothering to live as if it had. In this case I still have to have a worldview, but it would not be one that would take too seriously the prescriptions of the Buddha, say, since he derived his teachings from his enlightenment experience. Nor would I take too seriously most of what Paul has to say in the New Testament, since again he derived his slant on practical things from his conversion experience and sense of unity with Christ. I might be a humanist, thinking that the highest value is reverence for one's fellow human beings. Or I might be a Marxist and work toward the revolution and what I thought to be a better world. Or I might be a hedonist, pursuing my own pleasures and satisfactions. But even here I have a worldview: "Eat, drink, and be merry, for tomorrow we die."

So in addition to questions about the nature and effects of worldviews, which we pursue through worldview analysis and symbolic analysis, there are also questions of evaluation. There are, that is, questions about the truth of worldviews, and about how we would set out to resolve such questions.

What the Christian or Jewish or Hindu thinker presents as the truth of his or her respective tradition has to appeal to experience or to reasoning or to revelation, or to two or all three of these. And so we are brought necessarily to think about what experience can show and what reasoning can demonstrate and what revelation can uncover. The general reflection about these issues goes, as I have said, under the name of "philosophy of religion."

These questions of truth are normative: They result in conclusions about what we ought to believe and what we ought to do—in brief, they result in conclusions about values. Whereas the descriptive or scientific study of worldviews puts "brackets" around values, but sees them as facts whether we approve of the values or not, the normative approach to religion, whether through theology or philosophy, is a more personal and social matter. A person or a society must decide which values are to be favored. Thus, too, the normative exploration of worldviews brings us to ethics, and to moral thinking as a means of trying to decide what should or should not be done.

The whole field of the modern study of religion is filled with many pathways, and many kinds of flowers and fruits and hedges. It has some ancient plants in it, but many others are quite young. It is a fascinating place to wander and holds treasures for those who explore it. No one person can comprehend it all or travel through all of it. But the map I have just drawn may orient the visitor and encourage further explorations.

The study of religion and worldviews is a study of the realities of human life. Let us therefore now draw another map, that of the individual religions and worldviews that inhabit, and have inhabited, our beautiful planet.

Chapter

2

Worldviews: An Inventory

The world can be divided into a number of blocs. These have changed with the virtual collapse of Marxism in the former Soviet Union. Even in China, which remains Communist in theory, market forces have generated practical changes that in effect allow more liberty for people to practice traditional religions previously suppressed. Although in the early 1990s there are still communisms in North Korea, Vietnam, Laos, and Cuba, nothing looks anything like a purely Marxist bloc. In this new perspective we can look to several main blocs. They are as follows:

The modern West, largely Christian in background though largely pluralist in character, stretching from the American pacific eastward through Europe to Siberia, and from Norway in the North to Armenia in the South.

The Islamic crescent, stretching from Indonesia westward to northern Nigeria in West Africa, via parts of South Asia, and the Middle East and North Africa, and reaching northward into former Soviet Central Asia.

South and much of Southeast Asia, all with a background of Indian-
style civilization, comprising Tibet, India, Sri Lanka, Burma, Thailand,
Laos and Cambodia.

East Asia, from China and Vietnam, via Korea and Japan, comprising
the Chinese sphere of cultural influence.

The Latin South from the Rio Grande to Patagonia.

Black Africa and the Caribbean.

The Pacific region.

In addition smaller countries and cultures are embedded in
these greater areas, notably throughout the Pacific and in South
and Southeast Asia, as well as through the Americas and in Siberia.
These cultures are not exactly a bloc, but they are increasingly
becoming a force. Also, the main blocs tend to have outriders: The
West has Australia and New Zealand, for example; East Asia has
Singapore, largely Chinese; the Islamic crescent has Tatarstan and
Zanzibar, among other areas; and South Asia has the Indians of
Natal and Fiji, etc.

These represent the great tectonic plates of human civilization,
and when they grind against one another historic earthquakes
occur. And of course there are very important subsidiary cultural
fault lines. If we can understand these broader structures, we gain
insight to see more clearly some of the features that characterize
them.

The Modern West

By "the West" I mean those countries making up Europe, including
Russia, and part of its "near beyond," such as the Caucasus,
together with America and Australasia, which in recent times tend
to share not only a largely Christian and Jewish heritage but also
pluralism of belief and to some extent customs. During the twentieth century many of these countries succumbed to a certain mad-
ness, namely Nazism, Fascism, and Communism, and suffered both
from a rejection of the liberal and Christian and Jewish heritages.
The collapse of the Soviet Empire in 1989 saw not only the restoration of traditional religions and humanism but also the creation of a
more pluralist civilization from California via Western Europe as far
as Vladivostok. It also involved the creation of some newly indepen-

dent Western nations, such as Belarus, Ukraine, Moldova, Armenia, and Georgia. Three Baltic republics also reemerged; Czechoslovakia split into the Czech Republic and Slovakia; and Yugoslavia split into various states, namely Slovenia, Croatia, Macedonia (called Fyrom, in an ugly concession to Greek demands—no prizes for figuring out the acronym), and an enlarged Serbia, still carrying on the rump of Yugoslavia.

Varied forms of Christianity have traditionally predominated in this whole area. Protestantism has formed a great part of Northern Europe, from Finland to Britain, and has shaped North American forms of Christianity. It has also harbored modern Western democracy, free thinking, and the separation of church and state. It has in great measure nurtured the Enlightenment and of course industrial capitalism. For fairly obvious reasons the ex-Communist states have less ease with pluralism, and yet traditional religions have emerged vigorously, such as Catholicism in Poland, Orthodoxy in Moldova, Armenian Christianity in Armenia, and so on. Moreover, demographically these states have mingled populations often enough. So practical pluralism tends to exist, even if threatened by ethnic hostilities.

The Islamic Crescent

The Islamic crescent has its heart in Arabia, of course, now called Saudi Arabia in honor of its ruling family, Saud. It was in the northwest portion of this great peninsula, in Mecca, where the prophet Muhammad had his call from God, from which ultimately flowed the religion of Islam or "submission" to the one God or Allah. Islam spread speedily in the seventh and eighth centuries across North Africa into Spain and through the Middle East into Central Asia as well as India. From the eleventh century Islam penetrated more deeply into India, especially through the establishment of the Mughal Empire. Pakistan and Bangladesh are predominantly Muslim states today; but even the mostly Hindu Republic of India has well over a hundred million Muslim citizens. Malaysia and Indonesia are also mainly Islamic, the latter being by far the largest Muslim nation in the world. Also important are the North African Muslim areas, from where Islam spread across the Saharan trade routes. While Islamic civilization was once potent and glittering, in more recent times, especially during the nineteenth and early twentieth centuries, virtually the whole Islamic crescent came under colonial domination from the West, succumbing to the forces of

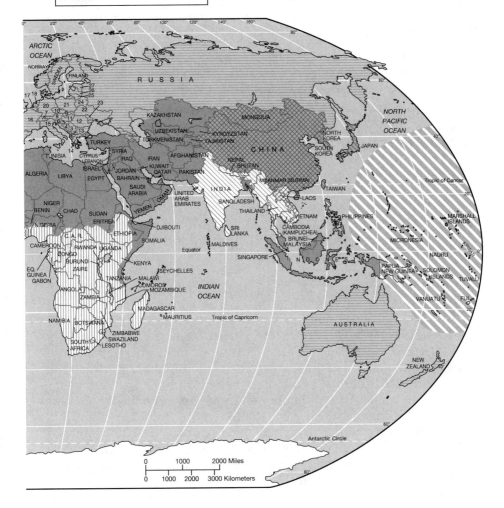

EUROPE	
1 ALBANIA	15 ITALY
2 MACEDONIA	16 FRANCE
3 SERBIA	17 BELGIUM
4 BOSNIA-HERZEGOVINA	18 NETHERLANDS
5 CROATIA	19 DENMARK
6 SLOVENIA	20 GERMANY
7 SWITZERLAND	21 POLAND
8 AUSTRIA	22 UKRAINE
9 SLOVAKIA	23 MOLDOVA
10 CZECH REPUBLIC	24 BELARUS
11 HUNGARY	25 LITHUANIA
12 ROMANIA	26 LATVIA
13 BULGARIA	27 ESTONIA
14 GREECE	

Britain, Russia, France, Italy and so on. In general Islam is divided
into predominantly Sunni cultures and Shi'i (often referred to as
Shi'a) areas, of which the most important is Iran, which underwent
a vigorous Islamic revolution in 1979. Other facets of traditional
Islam include Sufism, a mystical or contemplative form of the faith,
and modern revivalism, often thought of in the West as fundamentalism and sometimes referred to as Islamism. Though in no sense
a form of Islam, the Baha'i religion arose within an Islamic milieu.
In 1923, Turkey became rigorously secularist, though becoming
less so in recent years.

South and Southeast Asia

This region is dominated by Hindu and Buddhist culture emanating
originally from North India. Indian values spread to Indochina, in
the first instance from the second and third centuries C.E. In modern times Hinduism has become dominant in India, while most of
Southeast Asia has become Theravada Buddhist—namely the countries of Burma (or Myanmar), Thailand, Cambodia, and Laos,
together with Sri Lanka (or Ceylon), which over the centuries has
stayed in close religious touch with Burma and Thailand particularly. In India there are important lesser religions, such as
Buddhism, Jainism, Zoroastrianism—brought by Parsees fleeing
Muslim Persia—Sikhism, Judaism, and Christianity, which settled
in South India from very early times. The countries of Nepal and
Tibet have been deeply influenced by Hindu civilization, the former
with a mixed Hindu-Buddhist culture and the latter with a
Buddhist one, which in its unique Tibetan form also spread into
Mongolia. While China has asserted its dominance in Tibet, the
area retains its Buddhist and Indian connections.

On the whole, Hindu-dominated India has been highly tolerant
of its various minorities. It gave shelter to the Dalai Lama and his
Tibetan followers when they fled their country in 1959 after an
unsuccessful Tibetan revolt against Chinese domination. On the
other hand, Sri Lanka has seen a long civil war between the majority Sinhalese Buddhists and the minority (mainly Hindu) Tamils. In
Cambodia, after their takeover, the Khmer Rouge, with a radical
quasi-Marxist nationalist ideology, massacred some million or more
citizens, including many prominent Buddhists. Burma has been
largely under military rule since World War II and has pursued a
largely isolationist policy.

East Asia

The dynamic cultural hub of this region is China. Chinese civilization has heavily influenced Korea, Japan, and Vietnam. In China the traditions of Confucius and Lao-tzu developed, mainly in the first millennium C.E., into thriving religions. From the first century C.E. Buddhism began to penetrate into China, mainly via the Silk Route and later somewhat by sea. The eventual outcome was an interplay and symbiosis among the three religions of Confucianism, Taoism, and Buddhism. Confucianism and Buddhism came to dominate Korea until recent times, when Christianity has become important, especially Protestantism. In Japan Buddhism became the dominant religion, though in more recent times the traditional practices of Shinto were elevated to a state ritual. The nineteenth and twentieth centuries have seen the creation of a number of new religious movements, some of them Shinto-based. China has been influential throughout much of Vietnam, especially the northern half.

In the twentith century, China and Japan took differing paths toward real independence from the threatening forces of the colonialist West. In the years since the Meiji Restoration in Japan in 1868, the country had clearsightedly modernized, borrowing ideas, techniques and institutions from the West. Japan comprehensively defeated the Russian fleet at the battle of Tsushima. It conquered Korea and in effect colonized it. After World War II Japan pursued its goals not militarily but by economic growth, within the capitalist system, and was encouraged by the United States as part of its Cold War strategy. By contrast after the revolution of 1911 and the end of the old Imperial system (which had been greatly inept at understanding the nature of modernization), China's intellectual and religious traditions proved to be inadequate as an underpinning for a new nationalism that could reestablish China's old power. The middle classes, which could support some compromise between old and new, were not strong enough. China turned to the alien Western ideology of Marxism, modified by the thinking of Mao, to provide the framework for its revival. In so doing it sacrificed a great part of its traditions, and most of its religion—whether it was the Three Religions or folk religion or the minority religions of Christianity and Islam (powerful in the West and Northwest)—was suppressed.

In 1994 a similar imposition of Marxist values remains elsewhere in the region—in North Korea, Vietnam, and Laos. Taiwan has stayed independent of mainland China since the defeat of the Nationalist government in 1949 and has reproduced something of the ethos of old China; and for most of this century Hong Kong has remained a highly successful capitalist enclave. Substantial Chinese minorities exist in Malaysia and elsewhere, while Singapore has rebuilt itself as a Chinese-dominated culture with striking success in economic development. In the 1980s and 1990s China itself has experimented with a market economy and has combined quasi-capitalism with party-ruled authoritarianism.

The Latin South

While Central America and South America have certain things in common with North America, they have traced a rather different historical and religious path. Because the region was conquered primarily by Spain and Portugal (the latter dealing with what is now Brazil), it has been strongly affected by Roman Catholicism. The fifteenth- and sixteenth-century conquest involved the subjection, though not the complete submerging, of notable urban civilizations, especially those of the Aztecs and the Incas, and the domination of smaller-scale cultures. In addition, African culture came to be represented in the region. Because of its dominance in the Caribbean it is convenient to include this area as part of Greater Africa. In general, Latin America displays three layers of society: those of Iberian descent, those of mixed descent, and those of Indian descent. Because of the predominance of huge landholdings in much of the area, the gap between upper-class riches and Indian poverty is often striking. Partial socialism came to be the way of Mexico and some other countries. But Argentina and Chile, the whitest of the nations of the region, have settled into fairly vigorous capitalism.

Though traditional Catholicism has been the norm, there has been the growth of a vigorous liberation theology (a kind of blend of Catholicism and Marxism) since Vatican II (1962–1965), when many reforms were effected in the Church. Protestantism has also often been vigorous in evangelizing Latin America. Pockets of Indian religions exist throughout the region, especially in Central America. We may also note that there is a substantial South Asian population in Guyana, including both Hindus and Muslims.

Black Africa and the Caribbean

Although in part Islamic, most of Black Africa is a mosaic of relatively small-scale ethnic groups that either continue with their own ethnic traditions or embrace Christianity. In the Francophone region (much of Central and West Africa; e.g., the Congo, Zaire,

Mali, the Ivory Coast, the Central African Republic, and so on) the predominant Christianity is Catholic, as it also is in former Portuguese colonies such as Angola and Mozambique. In Anglophone Africa, which includes part of West Africa, East Africa and Southern Africa, the majority of Christians are Protestant. There are a growing number of independent churches throughout Black Africa, namely Africa South of the Sahara. We can leave out of consideration here that part of Africa to the north and east, that is largely Arab—Morocco, Algeria, Tunisia, Egypt, most of the Sudan, and Somalia. Ethiopia—except for a few short years from 1935 onward when it was under Italian occupation—has remained an independent Christian empire over the centuries, with ecclesiastical links to the Coptic Christians of Egypt. It has carried on a form of the faith known as Ethiopic. Ethiopia has proved to be a mythic magnet for overseas African groups, such as the Rastafarians, called after the ruler Ras Tafari (or Haile Selassie). The independent Churches, ranging from very small to having millions of adherents, often creatively combine elements from indigenous religions of Africa, or what may be called classical African religion, with the incoming missionary forms of Christianity.

At the foot of Africa, South Africa incorporates the Dutch Reformed traditions of the white settlers of Dutch and other extractions, known as Afrikaners. The British and others also settled there. Only recently, basically since 1994, have the rights of the African majority been given practical recognition. The system of apartheid, introduced in 1948 and rigidly enforced from then onward, generated conflict between progressive or liberal Christians and the more conservative tendencies of many of the white settlers. South Africa also contains up to a million South Asians, many of whom are Hindus. There are not only a fair number of South Asian Muslims but also Muslims from earlier times, brought over from Indonesia.

The new religious movements of Africa help to express something of the African spirit in the reinterpretation of Christianity, and allow Africans to exercise control over their identities as Christian and religious people. But other forces are also present in Africa, such as liberation theology and a revival of African values within an orthodox Christian framework.

Also an important area of black culture is the Caribbean. It has created various blended religions (taking elements either of Catholicism or of Protestantism and interweaving African myths, rituals, and values)—such as Voodoo or Vodun, associated especially with Haiti, and Rastafarianism, important in Jamaica. There is an increasing interplay between the New World and Africa, during a period of postcolonialism and of a rising consciousness of African roots.

The Pacific

The peoples of the Pacific comprise three main groups—the Polynesians, whose spectacular voyages brought them as far as Easter Island and New Zealand; the Melanesians of the Southwest Pacific including Papua New Guinea; and then the Micronesians scattered in the West. We should add to these groups the Australian aborigines, now undergoing something of a renaissance. Mostly the islanders have converted to Christianity, which has become the dominant religion of the region. Missionaries came mainly in the nineteenth century, some time after the great voyages of Captain Cook (1728–1789). The impact of colonialism and then World War II, where so much of the region was fought over, helps to explain the rise of various cargo cults—messianic movements heralding the magical arrival of quantities of Western goods.

In modern times there has been much interest in certain features of Pacific religion: such as the concept of mana, or holy power, among Polynesians; and the use of totems in Australian indigenous religion and the concept of dream time, a kind of sacred era from which many of the customs and rites of the tribe originated.

The Rise of Nationalism

We have now had a quick tour of the seven blocs. But there is a pervasive feature of modern life that I have not yet directly commented on. It is the growth of the nation-state and the ideal of nationalism, namely that every people should in principle have its own state. This ideal had its origins before the French Revolution, but the revolution had an especially powerful impact on it. Later, in the nineteenth century, some of the major European nations achieved unification and independence—notably Germany and Italy, but also Greece, Norway, Belgium, Holland, and Luxembourg. In the twentieth century the movement grew, partly because of World War I and the subsequent Treaty of Versailles, which recognized the ideal. As a result, Poland, Finland, Romania, Yugoslavia, Czechoslovakia, Albania, and Bulgaria achieved roughly their present forms. South Africa, Canada, Australia, and New Zealand had also become independent states. After World War II the movement spread to the rest of the world. The trouble spots of the latter part of the twentieth century occur mostly where a national group—the Turks in Cyprus, the Palestinians in Israel, the Catholic Irish in Ulster, the Basques in Spain, the Muslims in the Philippines, for example—feels that it does not have independence.

Nationalism is not quite a religion, but it has some of the same characteristics. Thus there is a deep demand for patriotic loyalty to the nation: Citizens have to give money to the state to pay for arms and for fellow citizens' welfare; they must, if necessary, be prepared to die in combat; and if they betray the state, they are branded as traitors and often shot. In the "monistic" states counterrevolutionaries are imprisoned or killed, often for apparently mild offenses.

The ideology of the state is also clothed in religious garments: There is a national anthem (solemn, it is hoped, and tear-jerking), a national flag and other emblems, and pomp and circumstance surrounding state events. These national events often include marches of ranked soldiers with formidable weaponry, for war is the great sacrament of the modern state, cementing its loyalties with shed blood, and weapons are a great symbol of collective machismo and pride. The state has, to a great extent, replaced tribe, clan, and in some ways even family, as the group with ultimate power over people's affections and loyalties. The educational system is one of the great shapers of the nation, often imbuing the young with common values through nation-building myth (history textbooks) and sports which foster group identity. Education is also a channel for the national language. For instance, in place of the many dialects of Italy's regions, standard Italian became the nation's language; English is the common language unifying the groups of different origins making up the United States. Problems have arisen among citizenry of nations that have inherited old colonial boundaries, as in much of Africa, where each country has within it a mosaic of ethnic groups and a diversity of languages. Often only the elite speak the official language (say, English or French) of the new national administration.

The national idea, then, has had a strong impact on the world. Virtually all the world is now covered by independent nation-states. Sometimes the national idea has also bred chauvinism and the desire of one tribe to conquer others. Britain gained an empire. The Nazis ran riot through Europe. The Japanese tried to conquer most of East and Southeast Asia. The Soviet Union in effect became an instrument for expressing Russian chauvinism, dominating the

Islamic peoples of Soviet Central Asia, other related folk like the Ukrainians, and, by proxy through satellite Marxist parties, most of the countries of Eastern Europe.

After the collapse of the Soviet Union, the reemergence of strong nationalisms from its corpse became evident. First, the European satellites such as Poland, Hungary, and Romania emphasized their independence. Czechoslovakia subsequently split into two nations, namely the Czech Republic and Slovakia. The Baltic republics regained their freedom, which had been snatched away in 1940. Belarus, Ukraine, Georgia, Armenia, Moldova, and so on demanded their independence. The countries of Central Asia also gained their independence. More drastically, Yugoslavia split into several nation-states, namely Slovenia, Croatia, Serbia, Bosnia, Fyrom, and so on.

It is important to see how religion and worldviews are often deeply involved in the national idea; the advent of nationalism represents a new backdrop against which religious attitudes and worldviews are thrown.

The various blocs are themselves in interaction, an interaction that is only part of the wider global interplay that makes the present era such a creative and exciting one. Now virtually every culture is in contact with every other. There are Hindu swamis in San Francisco. There are Samoans in Auckland, New Zealand. There are Pakistanis in Bradford, England. There are Turks in Munich. The major cities of the world—London, Paris, Singapore, Hong Kong, New York, Los Angeles, Lagos, Buenos Aires, Colombo, for example—have populations mixed in ethnic stock, in religion, in custom. Such centers are new melting pots and each is a smaller version of the coming global city. We all are more and more tightly involved with one another. It is characteristic of culture-contact that new intermediate social forms are produced. The great religions are thus increasingly liable to influence one another and to give rise to new varieties.

Such a state of affairs can also create a backlash. The Iranian Revolution is but one of a number of examples where a more conservative or "fundamentalist" interpretation of tradition evolves as a result of threats from various outside spiritual and material influences.

Because traditional religions often give the impression that nothing changes (it is often seen as the highest stamp of approval to say "This is how we have always done it," or "This is the same faith as that of our forefathers"), it is easy for us to underestimate changes that are taking place now and have in fact always done so.

At the present time every society is experiencing the growth of new religious and ideological movements. Thus, there are new cults in North America, independent churches in Africa, reform movements within Hinduism and Buddhism, and new varieties of Marxism. The process of religious and ideological change will likely accelerate as the world exchanges values in the marketplace of the global city.

Contributions of the Past

Any inventory of the major worldviews today ought not to neglect the formative traditions of the past—once great but perhaps now less evident. Looking back to the classical past of Western culture we find the religious thought that built upon Plato and had such a large effect on Christianity in the early centuries—the worldview known as Neoplatonism (literally "new Platonism"). Its main focus, a reaching upward toward the experience of union with the One, the first principle from which the cosmos evolved, has likenesses to some Hindu thought.

A group of movements at the periphery of the early Christian faith drew inspiration both from the Hebrew past and other elements of Egyptian and other cultures of the Eastern Mediterranean. That group of movements is now known as Gnosticism, because the adherents sought to be Gnostics, or those who *know* (from the word *gnosis*, knowledge); that is, those who know through experience the true secret nature of the divine Being. Sometimes their ideas took root in Christianity; the Gnostics also helped to cause that faith to define itself, partly by reaction against some of their wilder and more heretical ideas. Some of the themes from Gnosticism were taken up into the religion of Manicheism, which had a wide currency in the Middle East at the time of Augustine (fourth and fifth centuries of the Common Era). Manicheism stressed the evil nature of the world and the need to strive for perfection in order to escape from the body. Echoes of Manicheism were found in later European movements in the twelfth and early thirteenth centuries, notably the Albigensian movement, which the Catholic Church crushed as heresy and which had its main base in southwest France.

Also of some later importance in the formation of modern Western culture were the old religions of Greece and Rome. Something of the atmosphere of Roman religion was absorbed into the Catholic tradition, while the mythology, philosophy, and art of Greece were major ingredients in the fifteenth- and sixteenth-century flowering of European culture known as the Renaissance.

Important, too, were the ancient religions of Mesopotamia and Egypt that left their stamp on ancient Judaism in one way or another.

Many other religions that affected subsequent religious traditions have vanished: The great pre-Columbian religions of Central and South America, for example, and other mysterious civilizations such as that of the Indus Valley in northwest India. And even deeper back in the past are the marvelous cave paintings of southwest France and northern Spain. Here and elsewhere we see enigmatic traces of old cults whose meaning had something to do with the hunting culture out of which they must have grown. Scattered in Europe and elsewhere are such megalithic or great stone monuments as Stonehenge on Salisbury Plain in the west of England—such artifacts are now intriguing clues for those who nurture theories of ancient gods. But without written records, or a way of deciphering some of the early records we have, it is hard to make sense of old religions, for we cannot through the written word voyage into the thoughts and feelings of these ancestors. It would be like trying to understand football by looking at dilapidated and overgrown stadiums.

Twentieth-Century Secular Humanism

Such, then, is a rough inventory of human beings' various religions. But there is more to be said about the present. We have seen that one major bloc is dominated by kinds of Marxism, which derive from modern antireligious theory of the nineteenth century. We have seen, too, how the backdrop against which the various beliefs move about among human societies has been altered by the forces and ideals of nationalism. But, at the same time, there is a strong thread in the Western bloc, not merely of Christianity and Judaism, but also of varieties of humanism. Many people today feel that the day of traditional religion is past; the scientific outlook has no place for God, or for reincarnation, or for other central traditional preoccupations.

At the same time there is a process taking place that some have called "secularization." That is to say, in modern societies people increasingly are moving away from traditional religious patterns. Thus, for instance, in Western societies many people are concentrated in cities and suburbs, and no longer in rural villages and small towns where society was more integrated and in which religion played a pervasive part. Greater mobility—with people moving from place to place in search of better work—has the effect of making us less traditional and more individualistic.

What a person believes becomes his or her own private concern. Moreover, for many people the choice is no longer in a traditional sense religious. There are more and more "religionless" people in modern society. Even in countries that have been thoroughly Catholic, such as Italy, there is some drift away from Church authority. Religion remained strong in lands such as Romania and Poland, under Marxist rule. This is in part because when religion is oppressed it tends to rebound (the blood of martyrs, it is said, is the seed of the Church), and in part because religion—Orthodoxy in Romania, and Catholicism in Poland—is woven into the fabric of national feeling. Thus, at a time when these peoples wished to assert their identities against the Soviet Bear that loomed above and beside them, the forces of patriotism and faith were blended together in a powerful mixture.

But if people sometimes discard the old religions, they still have some sort of view of the nature of life. At its most articulate level this worldview typically is scientific humanism. Let us try briefly to spell out what this means.

As *humanism*, it believes that the highest values are to be found in human beings and their creations. But it does not hold that humans survive death or have any kind of immortal nature; nor that they exist because they have been brought into being by a God. Traditional Western religious doctrines and myths are thus rejected. So the word "humanism" is used in rather a forceful and exclusive sense: It means that there is nothing higher than the human race. Of the two great commandments of the Jewish and Christian traditions, "Love God" and "Love thy neighbor," the first disappears, and morality flows from the second. But such humanism is also in an important way thought to be *scientific*. The person who holds to this worldview believes that all true knowledge about the world is ultimately to be found through science, or at least within the framework of a scientific outlook. We know about the universe by telescopes and space probes, by mathematical theories and physical principles. We know about living beings by beginning with biology. We are, admittedly, still very ignorant, but by experimenting, observing, probing, and theorizing we shall get to know more and more. There is no room in science for God or for nirvana. There is still less room to accept things merely on authority, whether of the Pope or the Buddha or the Qur'ān or the Bible. Indeed, science flourishes best in a society that is open, where differing theories can compete and where people and education are not muzzled by ideological or religious orthodoxy. Scientific humanism favors liberty, a liberal outlook, and democratic institutions, and thus tends to be at odds with mainline Marxism. In some countries a form of social-democratic or liberal socialist outlook has been worked out that absorbs some of the thinking of Marx; but on the whole scientific humanism tends to be an ideology of the Western bloc, and has a strong influence side by side with varieties of Christianity and Judaism.

Humanism and Christianity have interacted in a number of ways. One strand in modern humanism, for instance, is the philosophy known as existentialism, expounded by such thinkers as Martin Heidegger (1889–1976) in Germany and Jean-Paul Sartre (1905–1979) in France. The movement owes much to the brilliant nineteenth-century Danish writer Søren Kierkegaard (1813–1855). Existentialism has greatly influenced modern Christian theology, but at the same time it has been a vital force in rethinking humanism. Very briefly, it centers on the following idea: Human existence cannot be defined or fixed—it is open to creative change, and this creative change depends on a new kind of freedom and authenticity of living in which the individual is not weighed down by the baggage of the past. Human beings have no essence; they do have, however, the possibilities of free existence. For the Christian thinker, truly authentic choice is found through Christ, seen as a person who, in his own day, broke through the baggage and entanglements of the past and of the ideas and legalisms of his time. For the atheistic existentialist, freedom is found in recognizing that there is no God who will help us gain freedom, and there is no sweet heaven after death; death has to be faced now, and life lived in creative awareness of it.

So in all kinds of ways we live, especially in the West, in an age of interplay, a flux of religions and worldviews, a new global city in which many differing ways converge. It is an exciting time. It is perhaps, too, a confusing one. But for all the novelties and the new philosophies we meet, many of the old traditions remain most vigorous. There is no way we can rightly understand our world unless we come to understand both those past great traditions and the new, emerging patterns of religion and humanism. Nor can we direct our own lives without giving some thought to the choices which the world now presents us. We alone can choose, but we now find ourselves not in an orchard where there is only one kind of fruit to pick, but in a kind of arboretum where the trees and fruits are many and beautiful.

The Structure of Worldviews

The various belief-systems of the world have different pictures of the cosmos. We might think of the structures of these views as a triangle: At the apex is the cosmos, at one end of the base the self, at the other society.

Before we look at these different views I want to point out that I shall use the word "cosmos" (rather than "universe" or "world") to refer to the physical universe. "Cosmos" is derived from the Greek word meaning "order," for ancient Greek thinkers were forcibly struck by the orderly character of the world they found around them—the sky, the stars, the earth, the oceans. "Universe" strictly means "all that there is," so if there is a God the word should cover both God and the cosmos he created. "Universe" often also more narrowly refers to the physical universe and its living contents. I think it will be less confusing to use "cosmos" when we mean the physical universe only. The word "world" sometimes just refers to the planet Earth, as when we say that the "world is round," and I shall retain this usage.

For the person who believes in God (the theist), the cosmos is a divine creation that reveals God's glory: I am a creature and I am made in God's image, and others are too. For the self there is the hope of salvation, a kind of blissful union with God, and for society there is the hope of founding somehow a divine kingdom on earth, a blessed society. I find my true self in worshiping God and in cherishing others. Such, in brief, is the way the Christian theist tends to look upon this triangle.

The cosmos is normally regarded by the theist, whether Christian or Jewish or Muslim, as having been created by God a finite time ago. The cosmos is essentially good and glorious, however much it may be marred by the work of hostile forces (traditionally thought to be led by the Devil). The cosmos is full of signs of God's goodness and of his purposes. This is so not merely because the stars and the mountains produce in us a sense of God's majesty but also because God's purposes are to be found in the unwinding of events. God as ruler of the cosmos was not just the creator of the world. He is also the power who continuously guides it and keeps it going. Those who think that God, having created the cosmos, is now detached from it all, letting the universe run its own course, are sometimes referred to as *deists*, a term for a type of Western thinker in the seventeenth and eighteenth centuries. It represents a style of thinking still found today.

For the theist, then, the cosmos is something that displays the creative power of God. But in many societies the cosmos is not the work of a single maker; rather, it has a more complex character. It has in it many various powers and beings that animate different parts of it. Thus, for example, the moon gleams at night as a sign of the power of a female spirit controlling and animating the shape-changing orb which we moderns know as a satellite of the Earth. The sun radiates heat because of the sun god. In the streams there are haunting spirits, whose silent echoes are heard every time we go to bathe or let the cattle drink. The groves murmur too (maybe) with the shadows of our ancestors. The thunderstorm exhibits the dangerous power of the sky god. So the cosmos is full of powers and gods, which are unseen but yet show themselves throughout nature. Such a belief-system, in which the cosmos is controlled by gods and other unseen forces, in the West is often referred to as *animism*, from a Latin word meaning "soul" or "spirit." Sometimes such systems are thought of as "polytheistic," that is, involving many (*poly*) gods (*theoi*)—as distinguished from monotheism. Very often such many-power systems also include belief in a High God, like the Roman Jupiter or the Greek Zeus, who is supreme but who, for various reasons, may not be so easily approached or dealt with as the lesser gods nearer to human beings. In any case it seems absurd (to many people) to deal with an exalted God about the petty matters that cause us anxiety here on Earth; so in some worldviews the High God is rather remote.

Important as animism is and has been, in many cultures it is fading for various reasons. For one thing, Christian and Muslim missions have made powerful inroads into much of Africa and the Pacific-area countries where such beliefs have been strong in the past. Although there are revival movements among such societies, the force of outside ideas is bound to modify them. Second, many of the older beliefs, long ago integrated into ways of life and methods of subsistence, are changing because of modern technology. The Eskimo settles into modern villages and uses new techniques of fishing. The nomadic herders of East Africa are often compelled to settle on limited territory. The Pacific Islanders turn crops to cash and benefit from tourism. The Australian aborigines work on cattle stations and accept social security payments. If there is an emerging ideology that seeks to refashion the old worldview in the light of modern knowledge, it is a kind of "environmental animism"—in which the cosmos is seen as containing powers and forces, including the human race, which need to live together in harmony. Such harmony is sometimes disrupted by the combination of the typically

Christian idea that the human race has mastery over nature (as though we were not ourselves part of nature) with the modern method of taming and exploiting nature. These methods are often shortsighted because, as we have already observed in our environment, such "mastery" can lead to the destruction of resources and the pollution of our surroundings. But important as "environmental animism" may be, the world of the small-scale societies is changing rapidly, and the belief in a many-power cosmos is fading from human imagination.

History has shown that the many-power cosmos has tended to be replaced by varieties of religion that transcend this idea or even replace it entirely with the image of a cosmos controlled by a single God. Thus, in Central and South America the old religions came to be largely replaced by Catholicism; earlier in northern Europe the old faiths of the Germanic and Celtic peoples and of the Slavs were replaced by Catholic and Eastern Orthodox Christianity. In India the various beliefs, myths, and practices have been progressively reshaped under the canopy of the Hindu worldview. In Southeast Asia Buddhism has found a place for the many powers, but strictly under the aegis and controlling surveillance of the higher doctrines of the religion. Through Indonesia and Malaysia, and in many other parts of the world, Islam has overtaken the older animisms, while in China a complex system of belief with Taoist, Buddhist, and Confucian elements has modified folk religion.

The world of many small-scale peoples has been one in which the cosmos is a jungle—the many trees representing the gods and spirits. When Islam or Christianity comes along the jungle is leveled, so that one Tree can be planted, that Tree which represents the One God. The old jungle may put forth shoots and seedlings, and these (the old gods a little revived) are the saints of Europe, Mexico, and elsewhere. Hinduism, however, does not remove the jungle; it treats the many plants as leading inward to the One Tree that is to be found at the Center. Buddhism, by contrast, though it does not remove the jungle, builds a road—the "eightfold path" that takes us to final liberation—around the jungle. Wander into the jungle if you wish, but it will not bring you further along the road.

If we turn to look at Hinduism we see a two-tiered view of the cosmos. On one level the cosmos is the body of the divine Being, and God, the second tier, is the soul which gives life to the whole cosmos. But whereas humans do not fully control their bodies (for what can I do consciously to alter the way my gallbladder functions or my liver secretes?), God controls everything. And while it appears that there are many gods in the imagination and the practical life of the ordinary Hindu, they are all seen as so many particular ways in which the one divine Being manifests her- or himself. But there is another level of Hindu thinking about the cosmos found in that system of belief and theology known as Advaita Vedānta—the non-dualistic (*A*- means "non" and *dvaita* means "dual" or "dualistic") Vedānta (the *anta*, or end of the *Veda*; that is to say, the final meaning of the Hindu scriptures).

According to this view the personal Creator who is the soul of the cosmos is not the highest reality. Beyond the Creator there is unity—the highest experience. The saintly searcher, the true yogi (or practitioner of self-control and meditation), is one who in his or her own soul realizes the highest knowledge: The self and the divine Being are one. In that state of unity and pure consciousness all differences between me and God disappear. The God who is "out there" and is the creator of the cosmos, and the cosmos itself become mere illusions for me in this higher state. I have gone beyond the cosmos. From this angle, there is a view of the cosmos as a kind of mirage, a colossal conjuring trick, or—to use the Indian word—*māyā*.

In this system of belief the cosmos is illusory; but for ordinary purposes the cosmos can be seen as the product of the divine Being and as being God's body.

In the Western religions the cosmos is thought of as created once and for all. If you stick to a literal interpretation of the story of Genesis, and the calculations of the generations described in the Bible from the first man, Adam, down to later times, then we can date the creation of the cosmos at 4004 B.C.E. (according to one well-known calculation, at any rate). Many Christians and Jews do not now believe in that date, but would still think of the cosmos as having been created at a particular time, now believed to be some billions of years back. Many modern astronomers trace the creation of the cosmos back to a "big bang," when an explosion occurred, out of which the cosmos expanded into its present form. But for the Hindu imagination the cosmos has expanded and contracted repeatedly over vast periods of time, for God does not create once and for all, but rather, after periods of quiet and passivity He or She recreates the cosmos. Similarly, for Buddhism there is no ultimate beginning to things.

Nor, in Buddhism, is there a creator. There is no single all-powerful God. Buddhism does not, however, deny the gods, as we have seen. They are reflections of popular ideas that are not to be dismissed out of hand, but they are not really relevant to the highest aim of living beings. With Buddhism we have a rather different picture of the cosmos: It is not the creation of God nor is it the body of God. It is a vast series of interconnected events, all of which are short-lived. It is a huge cloud of processes. It is itself without permanent substance. Nothing in it is eternal or changeless; its heart is empty. This "emptiness" is what the saint or the Buddha can see when he or she gains enlightenment, or nirvana. For the Buddhist the cosmos is a kind of mirage. Insofar as we think of it as solid, as having permanence, we are deluded. It is not actually how it appears. Everything is in flux, just as we are: I, however long I may wander through life after life of reincarnation, have nothing permanent in me, either. Only if I see the true nature of emptiness and impermanence, usually through a kind of inner vision brought about by following various practices of meditation, shall I gain liberation.

In China, Buddhism was affected by Taoism. In Taoism the true nature of the cosmos was summed up as the Tao, a word that has many meanings clinging to it—the Way, or Principle, or Method. It was used in particular to mean the Way of the cosmos, the principle or spirit governing it. Buddhism identified this with the emptiness that lies beyond the impermanence of things. The two ways of looking at the cosmos brought about that highly creative phase of Buddhism known as Ch'ān in China and Zen in Japan, both of which stressed the need for a kind of harmony with the true nature of the cosmos.

These, then, are some of the pictures of the cosmos found among traditional religions. In the case of theism, the cosmos is the creation of a divine mind. In the Hindu tradition it is seen either as the body of God or, alternatively, it is an illusion beyond which is ultimate reality. In Buddhism, it is both uncreated and impermanent. In Taoism, it is governed by a spiritual principle. In polytheism, many divine beings are in interplay, often under the leadership of a High God.

In all of these pictures there is some notion that by changing one's orientation or by being in rapport with the divine Being behind the cosmos, it is possible to gain mastery over it (in animism that mastery is rather piecemeal). In short, all these views are in some degree or another mind-oriented. They see the cosmos as wholly or partly the product of a supreme mind, or of our own mind.

In contrast, materialism in its various forms sees the mind as just a byproduct of the cosmos. The world was not created by God; God was created by us and we are created out of matter. There have been materialist philosophies since ancient times—for example, in India at and even before the time of Buddha, and in ancient Greece.

But in modern times there are two. One is Marxism, which, in its understanding of human history, gives a special role to economics and theories of material production. Marx thought that life arose out of matter, and in due course society emerged in a form that contained within itself certain contradictions or tensions. These tensions brought about a struggle between economic classes that helped to fuel the onward drive of events. But culture and knowledge were essentially byproducts of material relations. For Marxists, therefore, religion is an illusion. There is no need to postulate a God to explain change and motion in matter; rather, the inner contradictions in matter supply the dynamics for such change.

The second form of materialism, "philosophical materialism," holds that conscious states—the center of what we call the mind—are nothing but specific kinds of physiological processes occurring in the brain and central nervous system. This doctrine produces a worldview that rejects claims that God exists in a purely nonmaterial state, or that the human soul has a real, but nonmaterial, substance. To put it crudely: If God existed he would have to be a material being like ourselves, and so could not be the creator of matter. Such materialism is, like Marxism, atheistic. But it differs from Marxism in not having the special theory of history and economics that has made Marxism such a telling force in the interpretation of historical experience.

These different pictures of the cosmos are affected partly by the human search for the truth about what surrounds us and partly by the quest for meaning. The human being sees the cosmos as a kind of mirror: Can one read in its strange and beautiful features a reflection of oneself? What light can the sun and the stars throw upon the directions of life?

The varied worldviews as they come together in the global city pose vital questions about the future. Is human life to be exhausted in the struggle for material well-being? To what degree are we nourished by visions of the transcendent and of what lies somehow beyond the cosmos? What are the ways in which religion and science can live together, if in fact they can live together at all? How much will the traditional faiths change in their struggle to stay meaningful and believable to a world where human knowledge and technology are expanding so vastly?

From one perspective the different worldviews are maps of how to live. From another they themselves depict those powers in human experience and the cosmos that stir people to action. Figuring out their meaning is thus one way of coming to see what will happen in the complex emerging global civilization forming around us right now.

Central to the shape of traditional faiths, and central to the estimate of the spiritual power of human beings, are the patterns of religious experience which have irrupted into human life. To those let us now turn.

Chapter

3

The Experiential Dimension

When people think of the cosmos as the work of a great God it is perhaps partly because they reason that the cosmos must have come from somewhere, and its beauties and design suggest a Creator of vast intelligence. Or it may be that they accept the word of others—as found, for instance, in such tremendous scriptures as the *Bhagavadgītā* or the Bible or the Qur'ān. But it may also be because they have some feelings in their own experience of a majestic, terrifying, overwhelming, loving Being, a divine Reality. Indeed, if we look in the Song of the Lord (the *Gītā*) we find there the most dramatic account of how Arjuna, the hero of the narrative, is confronted by the Lord in all his many-formed glistening power, like a very personal nuclear explosion. And running like a thread through the Qur'ān is the sense of the experiences of the mighty and compassionate Allah who came to Muhammad and set him on his amazing prophetic quest. The Bible, too, echoes with a sense of the mighty presence of the Lord—for Isaiah in the Temple, for Job in his complaining despair, for the apostle Paul as he plodded along the road to Damascus, ready to deal death to the disciples of that very Christ who now suddenly blinded him and crashed around his scared skull.

Not all religious people have such dramatic encounters. But people frequently do experience feelings that softly echo these great turning points in human history. Indeed, much of religious ritual is designed to express and to stimulate such feelings. The soaring columns of a great European cathedral, the dim religious light, the high-flying solemn choral music, the sanctity of slow procession, the clashing of the mysterious bells, the dark features of the great judge Christ depicted in the wondrous colored windows: All these things are meant to give us the feel of the Lord, the feel of the numinous God.

And in the humbler chapels of Protestantism, which are plain and without all the expensive and highly organized aids to experience, there is the intense feeling of the hymn, and the thundering voice of the preacher. It sometimes seems as if the preacher is possessed by some force outside of him and beyond him. That is as it ought to be, for he speaks and thunders not in his own name but in the name of the Lord to whom he has devoted his life, and it is this Lord whose majesty and mercy he seeks to express.

One can get a sense of the numinous God outside the cathedral, church, or temple—in nature. Religious thinkers and believers have long heard the "voice of God" in the wind on the tips of the soaring mountains, for instance, or in the churning of the ocean.

And sometimes the sense of presence comes to a person for no obvious outer reason at all. So we find many instances of people who are awed by an unseen force that seems to approach them wordlessly.

Numinous and Mystical Religious Experience

All this is one important strand of religious experience for which Rudolf Otto (1869–1937) in *The Idea of the Holy* coined the word "numinous." This he derived from the Latin word *numen*, a spirit— the sort of spirit that in Roman religion haunted the rivers and the copses and strange places and the threshold and the hearth— unseen forces sending a thrill of fear and power down one's back. For Otto the numinous experience is at the heart of religion. He defined it as the experience of something that is a *mysterium tremendum et fascinans*—a mystery that is fearful, awe-inspiring (*tremendum*, literally meaning "to be trembled at"), and fascinating, and that, for all its fearfulness, draws you toward it. You get something of this feeling looking over a cliff. Doesn't the great drop inspire fear, and yet aren't you also drawn toward it, so much so that sometimes you have to make a conscious effort to draw back? But above all, the sense of presence that confronts a person in the numinous experience is majestic: marvelous in power and glory. In their rather different ways the experiences of Arjuna, Isaiah, Job, Paul, and Muhammad are all numinous in character.

As I have said, for Rudolf Otto this kind of experience lay at the heart of religion. Through it he tried to explain the meaning of the Holy, and he saw holiness as the key category we use in defining religion. God is not just good: He is *holy*, and religion, for Otto, concerns that which is holy.

Otto also referred to the Holy as the Wholly Other—both because it was something completely other than the person encountering it, and because it was mysteriously other in quality from the things and people of this world. It is thus *different* and otherworldly, a description that fits in with many accounts of God in living religious contexts.

Otto was attempting to depict the central experience of religion. Since feelings were involved in the numinous experience he thought that the reader of his book would not understand it unless he too had had such an experience—and indeed, empathy would require at least some inkling of the nature of numinous feelings. But I think most people do understand: Who has not felt awe before a storm? Who has not had ghostly intimations of a strange presence? Who has not felt dread? These may not amount to a full experience of the Holy but they are a step along the way.

Otto stressed feeling and the sense of the numinous because he wished to drive a path between physics and ethics, between the natural world and the world of value. If we go back to Immanuel Kant (1724–1804), chief figure of the European Enlightenment and the one who set the agenda for so much of Western philosophy since, we find a philosopher who wished to make sense of science— to try and see what the foundations of science are. But he wished to do this in a way which still left room for the moral agent; his philosophy recognized freedom of will outside the absolute constraints of the laws of physics. In so doing, however, it divided reality into two categories: science and ethics. Otto wanted to show how religion comes *in between:* It is in part about the cosmos, but it is not science; it is about action, but it is not just ethics—it is also worship. Worship comes in because the appropriate response to the Holy is indeed worship and adoration. Religion, in Otto's view, may also express itself as moral action, but at its heart, worship is expression of a feeling of reverence for the numinous. Indeed, a typical characteristic of religion is that it involves the worship of God or gods. But is worship universal? And is it always of central importance? Are there religions, in other words, where worship is only secondary? The answer is yes.

There is another kind of religious experience—mystical experience—that has been very important for the history of humanity, and that does not seem to have the qualities Otto ascribes to the numinous. Thus, in the Indian tradition particularly and especially in Buddhism we find the practice of yogic meditation, aimed at purifying the consciousness of the individual to such a degree that all images and thoughts are left behind. It is as if the meditator is ascending a kind of inner ladder where at the highest rungs he or she gains a kind of pure bliss and insight, free from the distractions of ordinary experience. Very often this higher state is spoken of as being "non-dual", in other words, it is not like our usual experiences. In ordinary perception if I am looking at something, say a flower, then I am here and the flower is over there. I am the subject who sees; the flower is the object that is seen. But this distinction between subject and object seems to disappear in the higher mystical states, if we can judge from many reports. Also, such an ascent of stages of consciousness is usually said to involve the stilling of all feelings and the attainment of a perfect quietness. This is very different from the dynamic and shattering experience of the numinous.

As we shall see, there are some problems with the contrast that I am here trying to draw, but the contrast is nevertheless an important one. To sum it up, very often the mystical experience that arises in the process of contemplation or meditation is non-dual, but the numinous experience is very much dual; the mystical is quiet, but the numinous experience is powerful and turbulent; the mystical seems to be empty of images, while the numinous experience is typically clothed in ideas of encounter with a personal God; the mystical does not give rise to worship or reverence, in so far as there is nothing "other" to worship or revere.

This theory of mystical experience as "pure consciousness" helps to explain why we find systems of belief in the Indian tradition, most notably Buddhism, that we do not give much importance to God or the gods but put the highest value on personal liberation. The saintly yogi achieves the highest detachment and serenity, typically as a consequence of meditation that brings him to a state in which no distinctions can be made, in which the usual world of objects disappears. At the same time, however, this purity of consciousness usually is thought to bring about a kind of knowledge or insight. When a person sees the permanent, the impermanence of the world of objects is seen; when a person achieves the highest welfare, the truly unsatisfactory and suffering quality of ordinary life is known. Gaining true serenity, a person can reenter the ordinary world with equanimity and know things and people in the new light shed by the higher state he or she has reached.

Thus it is that the central figure in the Buddhist faith, Gautama, left his wife, child, and luxurious life (according to the received story) to pursue the quest for the truth about the suffering of the world. After sitting at the feet of various teachers and practicing various kinds of self-control and fasting, he finally attained a state of enlightenment while sitting beneath a tree—the famous Bodhi, or Enlightenment Tree (an offshoot of which is still to be seen at Bodh-Gaya in northern India). He became thus the ideal expression of wisdom, who sought—and found—insight in the upper reaches of his consciousness, having tested in his mind various theories about the cosmos. As a result of his experience, he taught his new insight to a group of former associates, also yogis and seekers after truth, and spent more than forty years setting forth the doctrines and the path to liberation. Gautama did not teach worship. He did not speak of the Other. He did not prophesy in the name of the Lord. He did not put the mighty creator of the world at the center of his teaching and life. On the contrary, he treated with irony the creator god (Brahmā) of those who conserved the ancient tradition of the Vedas, the priestly caste known as Brahmins. According to the Buddha, Brahmā was merely under the illusion he had created the world—a mistake arising from the fact that after a period in which the cosmos lies dormant, asleep between two vast ages of dynamism, the first living being to rise in the cosmic cycle is the god Brahmā, who ignorantly thinks that because he is the first thing being to emerge he caused what came after. But what came after was already programmed to emerge, independently of Brahmā's activity. This irony about the great god is an indication of how Buddhism, while not denying the gods outright, sought to put them down, to show that they were at best of secondary value. In fact, at the heart of the Buddha's message lies not the experience of gods or God but the non-dual experience of liberation. Virtually all the later teachings and variations of Buddhism can be seen as so many different ways of captivating human beings, through religious myths and practices, to set them forth on a path that will bring them freedom. This freedom consists of an experience of "emptiness," or purity of consciousness, together with the perception that this emptiness is the underlying nature of things, that they are without permanent substance.

But another strand in Indian thinking is worth consideration and helps to open up the debate about the contrast between the numinous and the mystical experiences. In those mysterious collections of writings known as the Upanishads, which came into being about the time of the Buddha, there are some famous so-called identity statements. These say "I am the divine Being," and "That art Thou" (usually interpreted to mean "Thou, as having within thee the eternal Self, art one with the divine Being"). The key words used in Sanskrit are *Brahman*, meaning the divine Being or Power, and -Ātman, meaning "Self." The two are said to be the same. Now, if we spell this out in more concrete terms, what the Upanishads appear to be saying in such passages is as follows: "That divine Being which lies behind the whole cosmos, which creates it and sustains it and constitutes its inner nature, is the same as what you will discover in the depths of your own Self, if you will voyage inward through self-control and the methods of meditation and purification of your consciousness."

Here, in effect, the two strands of religious experience and thinking are being woven together. On the one hand, there is the numinous Brahman, seen as divine Power behind the cosmos and dimly visible through nature. This numinous Being in later Indian thought is portrayed in a more personal and dramatic way, as the great gods Shiva and Vishnu and as the divine female Kali, replete with power, terror, and love. On the other hand, there is the mystical search within. The Upanishads in a flash of insight bring the two together: The divine Being is found not only out there but also within the heart. This is a theme of much mysticism elsewhere—among Christians, for instance, who adopt the path of contemplation in order to seek God at the depths of their souls.

But in doing this such Christians are seeing the inner path in the light of a previously accepted numinous God who is the object of worship and devotion. In the case of Buddhism there was no such prior assumption: Buddhism was interested more in pursuing the inner path without believing in the Creator and the Wholly Other.

Let us see how far we've come in setting out a theory about the types of religious experience. Some religious traditions or phases of traditions stress the powerful Other, the great Creator. Others stress more the inner quest, without reference to God. Others combine the two quests. Before going on to see the questions that stem from this theory, it may be useful to see whether there are other strands of religious experience to consider.

The British writer R. C. Zaehner (1919–1975) drew attention, as others have done, to the fact that in a number of cultural contexts people may have a very powerful sense of unity with nature—with the cosmos around them. This sense of being lost to oneself but yet united to the world around, this sense of being part of a whole, Zaehner referred to as the "panenhenic" experience. The word derived from Greek means "all (*pan*) in (*en*) one (*hen*) ish (*ic*)." This concept may have been important for teachers of early Taoism. It came to be important in the development of Chinese and Japanese Buddhism, for instance in Zen, where themes from Taoism were blended with the spirit of Buddhist meditation. Thus, often we find in Zen art the idea of the disappearance of all distinctions between oneself and the world around one. The Zen poem—haiku—attempts in brief compass to bring out something of this strange and yet also beautiful way of perceiving the world.

Another form of religious experience, prevalent among small-scale and hunting societies, is that of the shaman. The shaman is a person who, because of his special personality, can make contact with the supernatural world. He will go into a trance and is thought to ascend to the heavenly world and to descend into the world of the dead. His ability to be in contact with spirits and his capacity to come back from the realm of death give him the power, it is thought, not only to tell where game can be found but also to cure disease. He can reenact dramatically the death and restoration to life of the sick person, and to restore him to health. Much attention has been given to shamanism by the modern historian of religions, Mircea Eliade (1907–1986), who saw it as a key phenomenon of archaic religion. This may be so because shamanism may have influenced early techniques of producing special states of consciousness such as methods of breathing and mind control in the Indian and Chinese traditions—and out of this came the whole yoga tradition. On the other hand, a strand of the shamanistic experience is found in the phenomenon of being "possessed." In trance the shaman may be "occupied" by a god and so come to speak the words of the god. He thus becomes a crucial link between the world of spirits and the community to which he belongs. Out of this strand of shamanism there may have developed the tradition in which the prophet not only is confronted by God as the numinous Other but also speaks in the name of the Lord as though he is, so to say, "possessed" by God. Thus God says to Jeremiah that he has "put words in his mouth" after mysteriously touching his lips.

So one model that we can propose about the way religious experience has developed is as follows: There are two developments of shamanism, which we might call the right wing and the left wing. The right wing focuses on the numinous experience of the Other, and the experience of the prophet is a special form of this. Institutionally, the successor to the prophet is the preacher, who tries to recapture something of the spirit of prophecy. The left wing focuses on the mystic or yogi, the one who practices the art of contemplation; institutionally, the successor of the mystical teachers of the past is the monk or nun.

This way of looking at religious experience, polarized into the numinous and mystical experiences, suggests that somehow mysticism is the same in differing religions, and that the difference between, say, the Christian and the Buddhist mystic is found in the kind of interpretation each places on her or his experience. Thus, the Christian finds in the light of the purity of her consciousness a sense of union with Christ, while the Buddhist sees the non-dual light as insight into the Emptiness, the Void, which lies in the midst of everything. But are the differences just a matter of interpretation? There has been much debate in recent times about this, for a number of reasons.

One is that, like Zaehner, some scholars think that there is a distinctive kind of mysticism that is different from the non-dual type (which he referred to as "monistic"). Zaehner thought that there is an inner experience the Christian and other God-oriented mystics undergo that involves the feeling of a loving relationship (he called this "theistic" mysticism). In this Zaehner was defending belief in God, for he thought of the non-dual experience as being at a lower level and so not as important or revealing. But once we talk about levels we usually are talking about value judgments. Why is the loving experience better than the non-dual one? It depends on your point of view. For many modern Westerners the idea of a personal relationship with God is at the heart of religion, but for the Buddhist we have to get away from preoccupation with personhood, which is only a mask of the ego, of selfishness. Who is right?

Another consideration is this: How do we tell what belongs to the experience itself and what to the interpretation? If I see a rope on the ground and perceive it as a snake and so become frightened, isn't it true to say I experienced a snake? So, if a mystic sees the inner light of consciousness as manifesting the divine being, does he not then experience God?

It may be so. But still, the idea of the single type of mystical experience is useful, for it enables us to understand that there are recurrent patterns of inner consciousness into which, according to context, people of differing religious and cultural traditions read differing messages.

This idea also helps explain some other things. It helps explain why mysticism in the West and in Islam has helped to promote what has been called "negative theology," or the way of thinking about God that stresses what cannot be said: God is beyond language, beyond thought. This side of belief chimes in with the experience of pure consciousness; if indeed God is found within—in what contains no images or thoughts or distinctions, in this bright and purifying blank—then God cannot be spoken of as this or that. This "negative theology" is a counterweight to the positive, sometimes very human ways, in which God is spoken of, for instance, in the Bible. Many preachers talk of God as though he is a human being, larger than life, who tells us to do this or that and worries about moral rules and whether there should be abortions or war. We should indeed see these important issues in the light of the highest values that we know, and for the Christian or Jew that means seeing them in the light of Eternity, of God. And since God is infinite, he has so much energy that it is not especially tiresome for him to worry about our minor human concerns. But even so there is often a need to counterbalance this human language about the divine Being with negativity: God may be like us but he is also very unlike us. He may be wise but it is not in the way in which a person would be wise. His goodness goes beyond all our ideas of goodness. And so on. Thus "negative" and mystical language helps to balance the other talk of God.

Also, our theory of two strands of experience helps explain a tension that appears from time to time between mystics and orthodoxy in traditions that believe in God. The orthodox stress the holiness and otherness of God. The orthodox Muslim or Christian conceives of God as Other and of us merely as creatures. It is blasphemous to put ourselves on a par with God. But if the mystical experience is, as we have seen, non-dual, and if by contrast the numinous God is Other, different from us, then there is a problem about the mystic's non-dual experience of God. The mystic often is led by the experience to say that he becomes one with God. He loses his sense of otherness from God. And this may even lead to the paradox of saying that one becomes or is God (as the Upanishads indeed say). This happened in the case of al-Hallaj (ca. 858–922), a famous Sufi mystic within Islam. He thought that all duality between himself and Allah was washed away and so said "I am the Real," using here one of the titles of Allah himself. For his blasphemy, for that was how the orthodox saw it, he was put to death—crucified, in fact, for he was an admirer of Jesus and crucifixion seemed a suitably ironic punishment.

Our theory of types of experience is also useful in helping to explain differing patterns of doctrine. If you stress the numinous, you stress that our salvation or liberation (our becoming holy) must flow from God the Other. It is he who brings it to us through his grace. You also stress the supreme power and dynamism of God as creator of this cosmos. If, on the other hand, you stress the mystical and the non-dual, you tend to stress how we attain salvation or liberation through our own efforts at meditation, not by the intervention of the Other. You also tend to stress the emptiness of things, the idea of a liberation that takes us beyond this impermanent life. If we combine the two but accentuate the numinous, we see mystical union as a kind of close embrace with the other—like human love, where two are one and yet the "two-ness" remains. If the accent is on the mystical rather than the numinous, then God tends to be seen as a being whom we worship, but in such a way that we get beyond the duality, until even God disappears in the unspeakable non-dual higher consciousness. This is the position of Advaita Vedānta, as we have noted; it is also in rather a different way the position of Mahāyāna or Greater Vehicle Buddhism (which developed out of early Buddhism and became the dominant kind of Buddhism in China and Japan) in its mainstream.

There is another way in which we may look at the distinction between the numinous and the mystical. In the numinous, the eternal lies, so to speak, beyond the cosmos and outside the human being. In the mystical, the Eternal somehow lies within us. In the first case we need to be dependent on the Other; in the second case we may rely upon our own powers, though the task of penetrating to the Eternal may be very hard. The numinous, in encouraging worship, encourages a loving dependence on the Other. The mystical, in encouraging meditation, encourages a sense of self-emptying. As we have seen, the two can go together. But there are differing accents.

In this discussion I have, of course, been oversimplifying. Because of the richness of ideas and myths in which experiences tend to be clothed, the feelings and insights people gain can vary subtly and widely in character. I have tried to combine Otto's theory with other theories which in modern times have emphasized the unity of mystical experiences across the religions. The famous writer Aldous Huxley (1894–1963) also emphasized such mystical unity. In his book *The Perennial Philosophy* he did much to influence Western thinking about the inner searches of Eastern religions, and so contributed to that flowering of mystical interests and gentleness that accompanied the otherwise turbulent 1960s.

Questions of Value and Truth

But a question is likely to remain in our minds. Is there after all any basis to these experiences? It is true that we may feel a sense of awe before the glories of the cosmos, or may from time to time experience a sense of the overpowering presence of God. It is true that yogis may purify their consciousness and feel thereby a sense of illumination and freedom. But so what? Could these experiences perhaps be delusions? Is the mystical, non-dual experience in the last analysis just a very interesting state of mind? And isn't the sense of presence of God just like a waking dream? We may feel that someone confronts us: Arjuna in the Song of the Lord may think himself in front of Vishnu in all his dramatic and terrifying glory. But is this not something that can be explained by some theory of projection? Couldn't we say that Arjuna projected his vision outward onto the screen of the world and then took it to be something real?

From one point of view we should not be concerned about what the value of various religious experiences is or might be. They have the effects that they have quite independently of how we may view them. But many writers in one way or another have tried to argue that religion is indeed a projection; and if this is true, it would follow that key religious experiences are also projections. The projection theory is one explanation of how so pervasive a feature of human history arose and how it maintains itself.

Consider one way in which the numinous experience, or one of its offshoots, is quite common in modern life: the experience of being "born again." The person who feels this, in the Christian context, often has feelings not unlike those of the great reformer, Martin Luther (1483–1546)—a deep sense of sin and powerlessness. These are the mirror images, so to speak, of the power and holiness of God as the Other. In the face of the Holy the individual feels unholy. Christ comes to such a person, giving a marvelous reassurance. If she repents, then the Savior will overcome the sin and give the person new power in her life. Some would argue that it is the circumstances of the person's life and times that created in her the sense of sin, and that the threatening figure of God was something projected from her unconscious out of a sense of guilt, arising from infantile conflicts in the nuclear family. To say this is to echo the thinking of psychoanalysis, going back to Freud's influential book *Totem and Taboo* (1915). Freud gives a psychological interpretation to then current theories of totemism in archaic religion, in which each clan or group has a totem or sacred animal, which is normally forbidden or taboo. So wouldn't we, by Freud's explanation, be suggesting that the sense of the numinous (with the *tremendum*—"to be trembled at"—aspect being played by the Father and the *fascinans* by Christ) comes from her own psyche, triggered by the circumstances of her life? If we could manage such explanation consistently, it would no doubt be a great advance in trying to understand the power of religion and the ways in which it works.

But for the explanation to be valid certain conditions have to be met. For one thing, Freud's theory on the dynamics of the psyche would have to be confirmed in a variety of cultures. Here there is a problem with Freud's *Totem and Taboo* and his later ideas about religion. He did not have access to the wide knowledge of other religions that we now possess. The fact is that his stress upon the role of the father figure in religion (which is, as it were, the heavenly image of the real-life father) is relevant only to some religions and not others. Moreover, the data which Freud drew on in late nineteenth- and early twentieth-century Vienna were largely related to a very special and not very typical society whose preoccupations were Christianity and Judaism.

For Freud himself religion was an illusion. His position has been influential not only because of the fruitful way in which he made use of the idea of the unconscious mind but also because his picture of human nature and the path of self-understanding became itself an alternative to religion. The analyst was able to take over something of the priest's role: He was a new kind of pastor, very much in the modern idiom. The new teachings of psychoanalysis could deal with guilt and promise a new kind of spiritual health. The patient, in undergoing the process of analysis, went through a new form of religious initiation and renewal.

This leads us to see a problem about theories of the origins of religious experience. Such theories may, like Freud's, begin from the assumption that there is no ultimate religious reality—that there is no God. So they already begin from a particular worldview—a humanist one in the sense in which we used this term in the previous chapter. But what is the reason for starting with that worldview rather than with one that accepts the existence of something lying beyond the visible cosmos? Or is there perhaps some neutral standpoint between rejection of God and acceptance of him? (Or between acceptance of nirvana and rejection of it?)

To spell out further the problem about the Freudian position on traditional religion: Isn't Freud using one worldview to judge another—like the Christian missionary we referred to earlier, who judges Hinduism from the assumptions of the Bible? Freud was—

with part of himself at any rate—claiming to be engaged in science. However, it is not scientific simply to begin with assumptions that would make a rival theory false before the evidence is properly examined. And once we begin to look at Freud's major writings on the origin of religion in the light of the evidence from the history of religions, we find that his theories break down. For instance, he thought totemism, or the worship of sacred animals, was a universal early phenomenon. He was relying on some contemporary anthropology that is now out of date. His idea that the leader of a primitive human horde had been killed by his sexually jealous sons was pure speculation derived in part from an aside in the writings of Charles Darwin. It is a remarkable thing that so speculative a theory should have won so much intelligent support in the 1920s. We can perhaps explain it the way many have chosen to explain the popularity of religion: It is a case of appeal, rather than truth.

I shall come back to the question of how we judge religious experiences, but first let us look at two further depth psychological approaches. One is that of Carl Gustav Jung, who broke with Freud in the early days of psychoanalysis and took a positive view of the value of religion and of the symbols people use in myth and ritual, the symbols that, so to speak, well up from the human race's unconscious. Jung's attitude toward religious experience was ambiguous. Although he did not affirm any particular religious doctrine, he nevertheless considered that religion could be useful in helping people reach balance and maturity, and achieve an integrated personality.

Erich Fromm (1900–1980), who belongs to the Freudian tradition, considered that religion could be a good force if it were humanistic. For him religion is unavoidable, or it represents for a group a common outlook and a common focus of devotion—and every group needs these. Fromm believed, however, that an authoritarian and rigid religion is bad for us. For one thing, all that is good and reasonable in ourselves is projected outward onto God, and we are left merely with a sense of sin and powerlessness. We are alienated from our own goodness.

It thus appears that from Fromm's perspective the numinous experience of the powerful Other is unhealthy. When he wrote about Luther (and Luther's religion was permeated with the sense of the numinous), he remarked:

> Thus, while Luther freed people from the authority of the Church, he made them submit to a much more tyrannical authority, that of a God who insisted on complete submission of man and annihilation of the individual self as the essential condition of his salvation. *Luther's*

*faith was the conviction of being loved upon the condition of surren-
der. . . .*

And this was because:

If you get rid of your individual self with all its shortcomings and
doubts by utmost self-effacement, you free yourself from the feeling of
your own nothingness and can participate in God's glory.*

There have been others who also looked at Luther from the
perspective of psychoanalysis, and there seems to be some ground
for thinking that the numinous awareness of God was able to play a
key role in resolving conflicts arising acutely within Luther's soul. In
other words, we have here a typical religious equation: a type of
experience that had part of its dynamic from factors outside the
individual, encountering the psychological condition inside the individual.

Luther's outlook, with its undue respect for power and authority and its sense of the complete sinfulness and evil in the human
being when left alone and without the intervening power and grace
of God, is, for Fromm, unhealthy. It is not humanistic, because it
fails to mobilize what is good in human nature. By contrast, Fromm
is more favorable toward the religion of the mystic and of Jesus as
he, Fromm, interpreted it. For Fromm, the Oedipus complex that
Freud saw as resulting from a child's sexual jealousy of the parent
is not so much sexual as a craving to free herself from dependence
on the parent. The adult, like the child, wishes to prolong childhood
and to avoid freedom. But a truly humanistic approach is one that
stresses freedom. When Jesus said "For I am come to set a man at
variance against his father and the daughter against her mother,"
what he meant, according to Fromm, was that the individual must
throw off the craving to be a child. Whether he is right in his feeling
for what the Gospel means is another matter.

Fromm's way of looking at religion is quite openly judgmental.
He distinguishes the good and valuable in religion from what he
regards as dangerous and unhealthful. As I have said before with
some force, it is important for us to look first not to questions of
value but to questions of power and meaning—to see how worldviews actually operate and what their significance is for human
beings. But if I may comment on the question of evaluation, then I
think we must look at religious experience in a wider context than
the psychology of the individual, important though this is. We need

*The quotations are from J. Milton Yinger, ed., *Religion, Society and the Individual* (New
York: Macmillan, 1957), p. 392.

to see the degree to which religion and its core experiences have been creative and destructive. Fromm, in writing the words quoted above, was trying to set the debate in a wider context, for he saw in Luther's attitudes some of the seeds of later Nazism. And it cannot be denied that sometimes the numinous and wrathful character of the experience of God can lean in the direction of hostility. Often the preacher "possessed" by the numinous also expresses hatreds. And, in particular, Luther was highly abusive of the Jews, and so contributed to that stream of anti-Semitism that was so destructive to Europe.

But on the other hand there are things to be said regarding the creativity of Luther the prophet. For one thing, Luther's revolution itself prepared the way for a critique of authority and for a new vision of the individual that has done much to shape Western culture. By a paradox, the human relationship with a powerful and merciful God can give the individual a source of independence against the powerful and often unmerciful pressures of the state, economic power, and prevailing values.

But perhaps the main thing we can learn from this brief look at some of the depth psychologists is that they too bring a world-view to bear in estimating religious experience. Their worldview is not that of any of the traditional religions. It tends to be humanist by denying the transcendent realm, the other depth that lies beyond the cosmos, which the older religions see as the abode of the divine, or of nirvana. The depth psychologists tend to start from a picture of the human being trapped, as it were, within the material cosmos. In so doing, they beg the question of whether religious experience tells us anything about the way things are—the question of whether religious visions and insights "tell the truth." If there is only this cosmos, then nothing, however dramatic in experience, will make us aware of something outside the cosmos. The experience of what transcends or goes beyond the cosmos will always be interpreted as having its origins inside us. So the question of whether religious experience tells us the truth at all is a question that depends in part on the worldview with which we start. It looks like a circle. But it is not a circle to be trapped in, for what it shows is that questions of religious truth are a matter of the perspective with which they are viewed. And which perspective—the humanist or the religious—is more convincing depends on a whole array of details.

Initially, in worldview analysis, we are concerned with the power of religion and its varieties of experience. One of the things we can learn from psychology is that personal factors will be important in determining the degree to which a type of religion "catches on." And depth psychology helps to explore how symbolic patterns, of which we are at best only half aware, help shape our feelings and actions and thus prepare seed beds upon which the differing world-views may grow.

Chapter

4

The Mythic Dimension

When the Christian Church was making its way in the Roman Empire it had to struggle against the Greek, Roman, and other religions, all of which had complicated stories of the gods. The Christians often spoke of these stories rather disparagingly, because they were not based (said they) upon fact, as were the stories contained in the Bible—particularly the story of Christ and his resurrection. The Greek word for stories was *mythoi* from which we get "myths." As a result of this Christian campaign against myth we still tend to think of myths as "false stories." It is odd, incidentally, how even the word "stories" sometimes gets this sense, as when we say of someone that "she is only telling stories." But as we have seen, modern students of religion commonly use the word "myth" in a neutral sense to mean a story of divine or sacred significance, without implying that it is false or true.

For the fact is that the stories of the Bible, which are in many cases historically based, fulfill a function similar to some of the stories about the gods of Greece and Rome and elsewhere. The term "myth" is used to highlight this likeness of function among stories in different religions or cultures. Thus an Indian text says, *Iti devā akurvata ity u vau manuṣyāh*: "Thus did the gods do, and thus too human beings do." This briefly conveys the thought that the myth of divine action presents an example of how humans should act. The gods are thus seen as paradigms. Likewise, in the Christian tradition the stories of Christ and of some of the heroes of the Old Testament become patterns for the faithful to follow. Other religions have a story of how death came into the world, and we are reminded in this of the events in the Garden of Eden. So in this and other ways it is artificial to separate supposed false myths about the divine from "true" stories as found in the Bible or elsewhere. There are important questions to be asked about truth, but these come later.

But we are, of course, looking at these matters from the perspective of the second half of the twentieth century. We have our own way of looking at stories, and we should see what this is before we consider the nature of traditional myths. As we shall see, stories remain crucial to our world, though they now have evolved into different kinds and styles from those older myths.

The Power of History

Of those stories, narratives, and dramas with which we describe human and other actions and that have special meaning for us "moderns," history is probably the most important. We seem to have a powerful desire to discover what the past was really like, and to try to piece together a coherent story of events. Interestingly, part of that desire to know about the past involves understanding ourselves and who we are. Thus, in high school we learn about our history—going back to the events of 1776 and beyond, for the story of our groups helps to give us a sense of cohesion, of belonging together. Think, too, how people like to trace their "roots."

In this we find two opposite tendencies tugging against one another. On the one hand there is the impulse to romanticize the past, to fashion heroes out of it (history as myth), because in a sense they make *us* greater. We draw substance from them. It is like ancestry: I think it is nice to be descended from somebody famous, for some of the fame then rubs off on me. But on the other hand, the dictates of truth and accuracy enter in. The modern historian goes on the evidence, as does the modern biographer. So sometimes our great heroes and great events suffer when the truth is revealed. It may turn out that our great leader in war was an alcoholic, or that some famous victory was the result of fortunate blunders rather than heroism and cunning. The fact that history is often about *us*, our nation or group, may encourage inflationary trends, boosting the "good" in it; while the more sober and scientific approach tries to be realistic, and may in fact seem deflationary.

Since the French Revolution, nationalism has helped to promote the writing of history as each national group tries to create, so to speak, its own past. It is now common to think of history in national terms—we talk of Italian history, American, Canadian, French, Indian, Cambodian, and so on—using modern political groupings to define the past. There was no consciousness as such of being Italian three hundred years ago. Different regions of the peninsula existed under differing rules. The German statesman Bismarck was not altogether wrong in referring to Italy as merely a geographical expression. But Italy emerged as a self-conscious nation and it is from this standpoint that we look backward to the "Italian" past. There is a strong trend in modern times to see history as a grouping of national histories, each of which illuminates the nature of the nation in question. In brief, the story of Italy or of the United States becomes a means of creating a consciousness of being Italian or being American.

So history is not just a matter of the scholarly investigation of the past; it also allows a people to form a national identity.

As for the tension, to which I referred, between history as myth and history as the result of critical inquiry, we might ask: "Why should we listen to historians who often puncture some of our cherished stories and rewrite our past?" The answer is that scientific history has authority for us. The properly trained historian can tell us how things were. He or she is part of the fabric of modern scholarship and science, which for us have an entirely convincing air. And this is where modern history is like traditional myth: Myths also commanded that breathless authority, unquestioned reality.

The tension between history as myth and history as the result of critical inquiry has become explosive in the religious context, where earlier histories tend to get rewritten. Nowhere is this more obvious than in the case of the Bible. Scientific and rather skeptical historians probe the documents that make up the Gospels or the books of Moses and cast doubt on some of the events there depicted. Did Jesus turn water into wine? Was he really born in Bethlehem? How did he relate to the people we know about from the Dead Sea Scrolls? We shall come back to these problems shortly.

Beyond the more particular historical narratives, theories have grown up in modern times by which such narratives are interpreted. The philosopher Hegel (1770–1831) had an ambitious vision of the whole of human history as a process he called "dialectic." This term could be translated as "argument," as though history constituted a complex debate or dialogue within culture, or within the human mind. He saw dialectic as a pattern in which one person affirms a position, called the *thesis*. Someone takes the opposite stance, known as the *antithesis*. Typically, truth lies between and beyond the two, and so a third position known as the *synthesis* emerges that takes up some of the points within both the thesis and the antithesis. This synthesis then becomes the thesis for the next phase of history, and so on. Thus, for Hegel, Jesus' religion was a thesis, Paul's the antithesis, and the two emerge as a synthesis, namely Catholic Christianity. This dialectical theory was an inspiration for Karl Marx, who translated it from cultural and intellectual terms into material and economic ones; so economic classes, for instance, came to be seen in dialectical struggle with one another. A middle point between Hegel's emphasis on the intellectual factors in human history and Marx's stress on the material factors is sociologist Max Weber's theory of how religion affects economic development, which in turn affects the shape of those religious factors.

Also we find in modern times some people such as noted English historian Arnold Toynbee (1899–1975) writing histories of the world. These are designed to let us see the whole sweep and meaning of the global past. These ambitious histories and theories do not please all modern historians, some of whom prefer to stick to the detailed examination of events rather than get caught up in speculation about great patterns of history. But the theories have had a great influence, nowhere more so than in the case of Marx's legacy. One reason for the influence of these theories is that we wish to "make sense of" the past in a way that may guide us in the future. In a way these theories are the heirs of the traditional myths that recount the drama of the human race.

But as important as histories and biographies may be, modern people look to other stories for illumination of the nature of human life—particularly literature and great novels such as those of Dostoyevsky, Balzac, or Hemingway, and dramas, whether on the stage or the screen. We have become used to the idea of finding truths about the world and about ourselves through what is for the most part *fiction*. Fiction is a category side by side with history, providing for us significant stories. In fiction and drama the events can become, by a kind of illusion, real to us. While we are in the theater we are gripped by what is going on. Within that framework of time and space, inside the theater during the performance, the story has authority and impact. Yet at the back of our minds we know that this is "only a play," "only a movie."

The Power of Myth

The myth is told or enacted through a ritual like a kind of drama and exists in an unquestioned atmosphere. It is uttered with the implicit idea "This is how things are and this is how things have been." Unlike history (although not unlike some theories of history), myth can tell about the future—what the end of the world will be like, for instance. Very often the story of the human race and of the cosmos is depicted as framed by "first things"—the creation of the world, the making of the first humans, and so on—and by the "last things" at the end. Thus the Christian Bible begins with Creation and ends in Revelation, with the final summing up of things and the judgment by Christ.

Not only are myths "given," that is, they are told with authority—a breathless air of unquestionable truth—but they also often play strange tricks with things and people. In the Garden of Eden there are a mysterious tree and a speaking serpent, for instance. Myths often contain a set of symbols, that is to say beings and actions with a meaning beyond themselves. So it is that Adam is not just a man, but stands for all men and women; and the action of eating the fruit has some half-known deep meaning that implies that by this act Adam and Eve are liable to experience death. Nothing here is quite what it seems to be; to decipher its meaning we need to look to what may be called "symbolic depth." In order to understand the mythic dimension we have to know something of the language of symbols in religion and human life. The work of Jung is fertile in this area, for he tries to give psychological insight into the kinds of symbols he found to exist crossculturally, in both the East and the West.

Because symbols are important in traditional religion, as well as in literature, where they find a new life, it is not surprising that religious art, poetry, and music often convey aspects of the meaning of life. Thus, a branch of inquiry in the field of religion is "iconography," the study of the visual symbols of faith. And secular worldviews, which most resemble traditional religions, also express themselves through art, music, and poetry. Thus Marxism produced socialist realism, a particularly heroic style of art that invests matter with a kind of shining light and in fact brings out the symbolic importance of production, revolutionary war, and so forth in the furthering of socialism and the consummation of human history.

I have spoken so far mainly about the "telling" of myths. But often myths are not just told in a verbal transaction: They are acted out in ritual. Thus, in the Christian tradition the events of the Last Supper are acted out in the Mass (the Eucharist or Lord's Supper). The story is conveyed in action. The myth is the script for a sacred drama. Many ancient myths are scripts in this sense, and it is no coincidence that Greek drama emerged out of the sacred enactment of myths. The old stories were given a freer and more secular form in the tragedies of Aeschylus and his successors. Some scholars earlier in this century belonged to what was called the "myth and ritual school"; they argued that myth is always to be seen in a ritual context. Although this point of view is too sweeping, it has been illuminating to see how creation myths in the ancient Near East (for instance in Babylon), were reenacted annually at the great spring festivals (for the spring, too, is a miracle of re-creation).

Part of our life involves putting celebration and the meaningful events of the past together. People celebrate my birthday; they perform what, in a broad sense, are rituals, like wishing me many happy returns, buying me a drink, eating cake with me, giving me presents. What is it all about? What is so special about the day of the year in which my birth once happened? Although the idea of the birthday is simple on the surface, it pays to look deeper. First, my birth is important because it is the beginning of me as a person (at least traditionally we have thought that way, rather than thinking about conception, for it is obscure and invisible, while birth is a dramatic entry into the land of daylight). My birth then is my beginning; and beginnings, "firsts" of any kind, we tend to think of as being especially meaningful—the Wright brothers as the first people to fly; the first time Everest was climbed; the first person to run a four-minute mile, and so on. The first of anything comes to stand as the origin of its kind, and so symbolizes the whole kind. Thus my birth is the first of "me" events, and symbolizes them all. Through my birth my whole person is celebrated.

What does it mean to celebrate? Well, first of all it is a case of *doing* things. Even the words that others use are words that *do* rather than words that *state* or *describe* anything. They are utterances that modern philosophers, following J. L. Austin (1911–1960), call *performatives*. They perform something. When I say "I promise," I am doing something, namely promising, which is a kind of contract. If I say at my wedding "I do" (take this person to be my wedded spouse) then I have thereby entered into matrimony. My status is in this respect altered. When someone says "Many happy returns of the day," he is not describing things (as if he were saying "The sun is shining today"). It is not a statement that can be true or false, but it expresses a wish, and in a conventional way it congratulates me on my birthday. This is congratulating me on my existence, and expressing the fact that people cherish me.

Similar thoughts apply to the performances that occur on July 4, say, or on the anniversary of the Russian Revolution. Here a piece of history is made present and celebrated because it is the origin of the nation or of the state. Celebrating American independence is celebrating America. This ritual expresses and stimulates feelings of pride in the nation.

Thus, we can see traditional myths as often providing the scenario for performances designed to do things—bring about actual results in the world. For example, the celebration of God's creation of the world may help (so it is, or was, thought) to stimulate new growth and fruitfulness.

There is one other aspect of birthdays worth dwelling on. Theoretically, any day could do, if all people want to do is to express the fact that they cherish me. Why choose the actual day of my birth? Well, of course it is not quite the actual day; that happened many years ago and happened only once. But we look upon the "same day" each year as indeed being the same as the day in the past when I was born. It is the day that occurs at the same point within the yearly cycle, to which, for various reasons, we attach great significance. In terms of position in the relevant sequence, the day is identical in position to the date when I was actually born. So we have the idea of cycles in which the "same day" keeps coming around. Because of its resemblance to the original day it is thought to reflect that day, and so my birth becomes present again. What is past becomes present.

This is a crucial feature of much ritual. It makes possible a kind of time travel from the present to the past (and even sometimes from the present to the future, as when in Revelation the events of the last days are experienced by St. John here and now). Thus at Easter Christians are aware of the risen Christ as being present to them not as an event then but as an event now: "Jesus Christ is risen today" is what the faithful say at the climax of the Eastern Orthodox rituals. "He is risen," not "He was risen."

One feature of the mythic performance, then, is that the events described become present. *Then* becomes *now*. But when did the events occur? Sometimes they seem to have a rather vague location in time, like those stories that begin "Once upon a time." As the

Gospel of John begins: "In the beginning was the Word and the Word was with God." But when was that beginning? Is it to be thought of as a date like 1776 or 1066, each of which is a "beginning," the one of the United States, the other of England?

The very influential historian of religions, Mircea Eliade, who was close in thought to Jung, has a special theory about the importance of the idea of "in the beginning." He considers that the prototype of myths is the myth of the formation or creation of the cosmos or of phenomena within it, such as death. The myth describes events occurring not in ordinary time, but in a kind of mythic time, or as Eliade puts it using a Latin phrase, *in illo tempore* ("in *that* time"). The Australian aborigines talk about a "dream time" in which sacred events occur. Eliade thinks that it was typical for early man to see things in his world as all the time reflecting that sacred reality "in the beginning." Jung would agree. For Jung the deep symbols or archetypes are present in the human race's unconscious, and they keep welling up into myths in differing cultures. Eliade makes the idea more specific in relation to the structure of myth. The myth describes the archetypes in motion: The ideas of new birth, of death, of wholeness spring to life in the myths of the first things. The telling of the myth recreates these realities and so it was that early man relived his deepest symbols. He overcame time and change by living in the light of "time that is not time," *illo tempore*. By contrast, modern folk have cut themselves off from these sacred realities and live in the shadow of time and change, the terror of history, as Eliade calls it. We are governed by deadlines, clocks, schedules—the apparatus of the tyranny of time.

Similarly, in his studies of yoga and shamanism, Eliade sees the experiences a person attains through various techniques as taking her or him beyond ordinary time. Time is annihilated and so the person comes in contact with sacred reality.

There are actually many different kinds of sacred stories, and not all fit into the pattern of events in "dream time," "*that* time"— which is not quite historical or "our" time. For instance, the story of Exodus in which the people of Israel were saved from their oppressors through the guidance of their Lord—an event celebrated at Passover and at other times in the Jewish year—is meant to be about an actual time in the past. Another example is the story of Jesus' death and resurrection, which the Apostles' Creed of the Christian Church cites as being very dateable, "under Pontius Pilate." If we look East, to the story of the Buddha's enlightenment, again we see an event of sacred and liberating significance that took place at a particular time and in a special location.

It is perhaps wise to pause here to look at some of the most important kinds of traditional myths.

Some explain the origin of the cosmos as a creation, usually by the thought or the word of a divine Being. Some tell of the emergence of the cosmos out of some preexisting chaos or undifferentiated matter. For instance, in some ancient Indian myths the world is conceived of as an egg; the splitting apart of the egg gives rise to the cosmos. Others see the cosmic order as a result of the dismemberment of a primeval human being, or a sea monster (like Tiamat in ancient Near Eastern myth). Water often plays a vital part because, as many studies have shown and as we have seen, water in numerous cultures is the symbol of chaos. Out of chaos comes order, the cosmos itself. Although the Genesis story, which is woven together out of various myths, has been put together in order to show in the most striking possible way the creation of the world out of nothing, and by the sovereign decision of God, here too we have reference to an earlier "something"—the waters over which the spirit of God brooded, and that symbolize a primeval chaos.

The stories of the beginning or emergence of the cosmos are one variety of a major and vital category of myths namely those that tell about origins—for instance, how an institution (like keeping the Sabbath) arose, or how a particular kind of plant or animal came into being. Important in particular are those stories dealing with the origin of death. Here is a fine example of this type, which Mircea Eliade quotes in *From Primitives to Zen*, from Sulawesi in Indonesia: In the beginning the sky was close to the earth. One day the creator God let down a stone on the end of a rope, but the first men and woman refused it and wanted something else. So he let down a banana, which they eagerly accepted. Then God told them that because they had refused the stone and taken the banana they would be like the latter. Whereas the stone does not change, a banana plant dies while its offspring continue. This then is how death came into the world.

There are a large number of symbolic themes here. The idea that the sky, the divine home, is close to the earth, the human race's home, suggests that there is not an alienation between humans and God in the beginning, but they exist in a much closer relationship. The notion that the first man and woman's action affects the rest of their race ties in with a common theme that the symbolic first being not only represents but somehow sums up in his or her own person the rest of the race. The fact that the first humans did not know what they were doing in choosing the attractive and edible banana suggests that God tricked them; this is in line with the belief that immortality is a divine thing and not for human beings to aspire to. The idea that what they choose is what they come to resemble (especially since in eating the banana they would somehow assimilate its essence) is a common one in mythic and symbolic thinking: Like affects like.

The idea that the sky and earth were once close is linked to a common theme in which the High God withdraws upward, perhaps as a result of some stupidity or offense on the part of the first humans. After that the High God leaves the real work of shaping and guiding the affairs of the cosmos to lesser gods.

Themes of destruction are also important and thus in some worldviews there are periodic creations and destructions of the world (this is most developed in the Indian tradition). Among cataclysms are great floods that are spoken of in a variety of cultures. Sometimes the theme of disaster ties in with the forecast of a period of peace and bliss to follow—hopes that, in a number of religions, have helped to inspire revival movements and sometimes rebellion.

There are all kinds of myths telling of the exploits of the gods, heroes, and other supernatural beings who control and infest the cosmos and surround human life. These are often the material for great epics, as in the Indian and Greek traditions.

Although it is true that stories about origins are important in the field of myth, they are not the only type. In this respect Eliade exaggerates, and he also perhaps makes too much of the theme of "in that time." Not all myths stress that there is something timeless out of which time-bound things came.

Still, Eliade and Jung attempt to show how the world of archaic myth remains relevant to us today—that the symbolic themes appearing in myths are rooted deep in the human psyche and perception of the world. A major way in which Eliade has helped to illuminate myth is by making us take seriously the manner in which time and space symbolize so much in our world. Thus the whole pattern of our thought about height and depth, center and periphery, shows something of our almost instinctive orientation to the world. And it is no coincidence to find so many myths that portray a mountain, with the upper reaches the abode of the gods or God, as at the center of the world—Mount Olympus in ancient Greece, Mount Zion in Israel, Mount Meru in the Indian tradition.

But although we can recognize how myths have traditionally played a vital part in fashioning a worldview (in fact the worldviews of many small-scale societies are expressed predominantly through myths), there are now limits on their credibility. They no longer seem to speak with that breathless air of authority, and once they lose this they cease to be living myths and become curiosities, tales, plots for dramas and movies, perhaps, the raw material for speculation about human symbol-systems. Is it not the case that secular stories, such as the theories of history we alluded to earlier, replace the traditional myths? And do not fiction and drama now offer an alternative to the older myth telling?

Still, there is a place where the traditional mythic forms live on in a vigorous way: in the scriptures of the great living religions. Once myths are taken out of the lips and hands of the storyteller and organized into scriptures, they have a new and different life. Thus, the Bible for the Jew or the Christian, the Qur'ān for the Muslim, the Lotus Sutra for many Mahāyānists, the Vedas and *Gītā* for Hindus, the Book of Mormon for the Mormons—these and other sacred and revealed writings have a life of their own in inspiring those faithful who look to them for guidance. They are stories that are given the stamp of authority by God or the Buddha or another High God, and they are preserved in a form that invites interpretation and commentary. In fact, these works often become significant to us through the commentaries. For one thing, commentaries often enable us to understand the doctrinal underpinnings of myth. Thus, if we look at a myth of creation by itself it may seem rather simple-minded: If God made the world, we ask, what out of? But doctrine helps to give sense to the idea that the world developed out of the divine Being himself, or that it was created out of nothing, since the divine Being experiences no limitations but can do anything. In effect what happens in the major religions is that the myth comes to exist alongside of and in interaction with the more abstract ideas of the doctrinal dimension.

For the most part, then, the dominant traditional myths now find their authority and their location in sacred books. New religious movements of the modern period accordingly create their own scriptures—such as the Book of Mormon, the Unification Church's Divine Principle, and so on. And it is precisely because these myths have been so recorded and preserved that they are open to the scrutiny of modern historical scholarship. When the myths themselves take the form of historical narratives, whether about Moses, Jesus, Muhammad, or other great founding figures, then the same tension that we spoke about earlier in relation to national histories should arise even more acutely here. Will modern history puncture some of our cherished beliefs? Once the critical historian looks on scriptures as mere documents, will their authority not come into question?

The Interpretation of Myth

There has come about, in the last hundred and fifty years or so, the modern study of the New Testament, where the problems of history and myth are most acute. The main documents of the early Church, and in particular the Gospels, were selected from a wide and growing range of writings that tried to interpret the life and message of Jesus. But they were selected not primarily as biographies or pieces of historical writing. The Gospels were meant to present the authentic Jesus of Christian experience and were to be used in the course of worship, as they still are. Also, they were clothed in the language of the day (the Hellenistic Greek understood in much of the eastern part of the Roman Empire—maybe Jesus understood it, in addition to his native Aramaic) and in the metaphors of the age. Those who wish to stay loyal to the tradition may want to restate the message of the Gospel in different language for today.

Take two examples. When the New Testament says that Jesus ascended into heaven, do we think of him as literally going upward? Thanks to science and technology, we now have an idea about what "up there" is like, which was not available to the original writers and hearers of the Scriptures. They thought of a three-decker universe— heaven above, the earth here, and the underworld below. Did Jesus go up like a modern rocket? Where is heaven—after you have gone up twenty or a hundred or a thousand or a million miles? In the older mythic sense, it was easy to think of the sky as being where God lives. Even if we think of heaven in terms of its being "the place where God is," our view of the cosmos, our cosmology, has altered. So how do we express what those writers and hearers were trying to say and think? Do we want to say that God exists, as it were, in a fourth or fifth dimension, outside space and time, yet always near us?

Let us consider another example. The Bible says that God is king, or like a king. The imagery of the kingdom of God is very strong. In those days kings had real power, but they do not today. At best they are constitutional monarchs, like the Queen of England—rich, full of prestige, a vibrant symbol, but without any genuine political power. The nearer equivalent to the old kingship is the U.S. presidency. So do we now say "God is our President"? If we simply use the actual language of the past, then, since meanings and circumstances have changed, the language now has a different force. So if you stick to the literal letter of the Bible you may be changing the meaning of what it was saying, is saying.

These problems of translating in order to reveal and express the original meaning are referred to as the study of *hermeneutics*. This derives from a Greek word for interpretation, and ultimately from the name *Hermes*, Greek god of messages. Hermeneutics is the theory of interpretation.

The modern probing of the New Testament as history has caused some arguments. Some feel that this secular approach to the text damages the authority of the Bible; they wish to reaffirm the unerring character of the text because it is inspired by God. Others feel that in order to be at home in the modern world we must arrive at a new understanding of the Bible that would take modern scholarship into account. The former are rather loosely called "fundamentalists"; the latter are often called "liberals." The fundamentalists too, of course, have a hermeneutical problem, for when they take the Bible at face value, aren't they reading the text with the eyes of twentieth-century people? And in doing so aren't they reading a lot of today's attitudes into the Bible?

Perhaps the most influential attempt to come to terms with the challenge of modern probings is that of Rudolf Bultmann (1884–1976). He introduced a program of what he called "demythol-ogization." This means trying to see what the mythic and symbolic language of the Bible conveys, and then restating it without the mythological clothing of the original text. Thus, as we have noted, the Bible treats the universe as having three levels—heaven above, earth, and hell below. This picture is now at best just a metaphor, for how can we literally go "down" to hell? For Bultmann this three-decker universe no longer fits modern feeling or thought. We now see ourselves differently, on a blue- and white-clad sphere, the beautiful planet Earth, swimming in space around a star near the periphery of a galaxy in a huge and expanding cosmos which teems with galaxies. This picture is beyond anything the Jews of Jesus' day imagined. But it does not mean that we have to abandon the idea that Jesus brought something extraordinary into the world, and that he is the central figure in God's unfolding revelation of himself to human beings. These are the Christian claims. Here we must remember that Bultmann is not writing as a historian of reli-gion, but more as a Christian theologian; that is, one who is trying to express and clarify in intellectual terms the Christian faith. But he has important things to say which are of great interest to the worldview analyst and student of religions.

Bultmann had to face the question of how we are to state the Christian faith once we have gotten rid of those mythic elements he thought modern folk could not accept—miracles like turning water into wine, walking on the water, casting out devils, ascending into heaven, being born of a virgin through a miraculous conception, and so forth. In order to explain the true and inner meaning of these mythic representations of the truth about Jesus, he went to modern philosophy. Bultmann saw Christ's resurrection as enabling the Christian to participate in a new and authentic way of life. This new freedom cuts through the false values which stem from treating persons as objects and ourselves as members of the crowd. Although science can deal with the world of things and so can be objective, the personal dimension of existence has a different nature. When I truly talk to *you*, you are no longer a thing or a type, but a person who responds. Thus, too, with the human being's relationship to God: It is a relationship of love, and what the Jewish thinker Martin Buber (1878–1965) called the I-Thou encounter. Myths in part reveal the personal nature of God, for they deal with the material world as shot through with spiritual and miraculous powers; but they also can be taken "objectively," as though they are just about objects and events, and not about what they are pointing to. Faith is personal and is a relationship to a Person. It does not arise from belief in mere outer events, however objectively wonderful.

Whether it is possible to accept Bultmann's rather sharp differentiation between the objective and the subjective, and between science and faith, is open to debate. There is also some question as to whether his modern talk of living authentically really gets to the heart of what the Gospel writers meant. But his project of restating the Christian faith is interesting, for it poses questions of deep importance for us if we want to estimate correctly the power and future of traditional religious worldviews.

First, the rise of modern scientific and technical thought means that most of those who accept traditional myth are compelled, in one way or another, to make a distinction between the language of faith and that of science—between differing spheres of human experience and understanding. Bultmann does this in terms of the spheres of persons and of things. The bible, in the last resort, is about persons and about God, the supreme Person; it is not a textbook of biology or of physics. So the myth of creation is about our relationship to God as our Father; it is not meant to be a material account of how the cosmos evolved.

But if we begin to make a sharp divide between myth and science, we already have a different frame of mind from that of the original myth makers. The myths now have a new context, and so a new meaning. Our world has already been split up into differing compartments, and it needs some kind of theory to put the compartments together. In earlier days Christianity had a similar problem in the face of Greek philosophy. For Bultmann the theory is supplied by modern philosophy. So Christian faith has to be given a rather abstract framework, and explained through such terms as "authentic" and "personal existence."

Which brings us to a second thought about myth. If we are to follow Eliade and Jung, the ultimate meaning of myths has to do with deep impulses in our psyches. They have to do with how we can come to terms with our feelings, and how we can achieve personal integration and wholeness. For Bultmann, too, faith is a very personal and individual affair. But traditionally myth has a much more communal meaning. A myth is not just about me: It is about us. Thus in the Bible we have the story of how the children of Israel came to be and how they entered into a special relationship to God. Tribal myths deal not just with the creation of the cosmos, but with the creation or emergence of the tribe. This is where national histories resemble traditional myths. We should not, of course, underestimate the importance of the personal and individual side of religion. It is very relevant to the modern world. But it is also good to recognize that religion needs to make sense of the history of the human race. It needs to give an account of where we are and where we are going. The attraction of Marxism is that it provides such an account. For the most part, Christianity and other religions have tended not to interpret the times, and so have not seen the meaning of the human race's transition to modernity and the emergence of the global city. There are exceptions, however. The French Jesuit Teilhard de Chardin (1889–1955) created a picture of the evolutionary process leading up to the human race as we now know it, and beyond to a new and higher unity of the planet bound together by perfect love, which he saw in Christian terms as the coming of Christ. His vision was an attractive one to many traditional Christians because it brought science and faith together in a new way. Evolution was God's mechanism for spiritual progress. But the vision was also regarded as going beyond orthodox Catholic teaching, and his writings were for that reason condemned by the Church. He raised an important question, however: What accounts of the past and the future are capable of gripping us in this modern and more skeptical period? What myths have the air of authority, the "reality" that makes us believe them, and not just treat them as interesting and perhaps insightful ways of conveying meanings in a poetic way?

The fact is that human beings have the impulse to find out who they are by telling a story about how they came to be. Myth thus is the food that feeds our sense of identity. And when we see our identity and our destiny in relation to the unseen world—God or the dharma or the Tao or nirvana—then myth is given an added impulse, for we imagine the invisible through the visible and give life to our faith through symbols. They are thrown up at the point where our feelings and the cosmos intersect, just as myths that give us a past and a future arise at the point where I intersect with my fellow human beings.

Chapter

5

The Doctrinal Dimension

Religious and other worldviews nourish certain kinds of experience. They find part of their meaning in stories about the past and about the future, but because they are views about the world, and about the whole of life, they rapidly develop a strong doctrinal aspect. We have seen how Bultmann tried to make old Christian myth relevant by reinterpreting the Bible in light of modern German philosophy. If we look back in the Western tradition, we see how the Church tried to make sense of the varied ideas in Scripture and ceremony about God, Christ, and the Holy Spirit by formulating that central doctrine known as the Trinity doctrine, in which God is depicted as both three and one: one God but having three modes of being—Father, Son, and Holy Spirit. If we look toward Buddhism we see that the nature of existence is summed up by the three doctrines (the three marks of existence): Everything in the world is impermanent; everything is without self; and everything is full of suffering, or more accurately, "illfare." If we look to the Hindu tradition, we see a number of differing systems of thought about the true nature of the divine Being—systems known as Vedānta. In Marxism, the interpretation of the onward dialectical patterns of history depends upon a view of the cosmos as being made up just of matter (hence the name "dialectical materialism" for Marxist doctrine).

Functions of Doctrine

The doctrinal dimension has various functions. One is to try to bring order into what is given by revelation, and in story form, in the biblical narrative. This is true of the Trinity doctrine. The need for order, in this case, had to do with the tensions that existed in Christianity as a new religion arising out of a Jewish background. Early Christians found themselves worshiping Christ. They did not follow him merely because he had been an influential leader. He was not just a Socrates or a Plato, a great teacher. He was seen as the risen Lord; the central ritual of Christianity, the Lord's Supper, focused on him and on his capacity to save those who had faith in him. So he was seen in some sense as divine. Yet at the same time Christianity was firmly Jewish, believing in just one God. Christians, like Jews, refused to acknowledge the divinity of the Roman emperor, and so were often persecuted as subversive. Their refusal was a sign of their strict belief in one God, in monotheism. But Christ too was God. How were these things—belief in the Creator God and belief in Jesus Christ—to be put together consistently? The Trinity doctrine tried to do this, and to present the plurality and the oneness of God. So one function of doctrines is to bring order into the material supplied by tradition.

Another function of doctrines is to safeguard the reference myths have to that which lies Beyond, to that which transcends the cosmos. It might be easy to think of the stories handed down in a tradition as being about supernatural beings who simply inhabit the world as if the God of the Old Testament dwelt in a whirlwind or a pillar or cloud, or Krishna were just a miraculous human figure who trod the streets and meadows of Brindaban in North India. Doctrines stress that there is something universal in and behind such figures, that God lies "behind" and "within" all events in the world, that he is somehow "beyond" the whole cosmos and is not bound to a single little part of it. These things are said through images and symbols in scripture, myth, and ritual; they are said more systematically in the form of doctrines.

Another reason why religions have doctrine is that they need, as we have seen, to relate their claims to the current knowledge of the age. Thus, in the early centuries the Christian Church found itself in a Roman world in which Greek culture and philosophy were the prevailing intellectual influences. If people wanted to understand reality they tended to go to Plato and Aristotle, as they might now go to science. But Plato and Aristotle were "pagans," or at any rate, pre-Christian. Somehow the Church had to come to terms with them. There were those who echoed the Christian writer Tertullian (?160–220) when he said, "What has Athens to do with Jerusalem?" (as if someone today were to say "What has M.I.T. to do with Christianity?"). But it was not really possible to seal off the world of Christian faith from the wider world of human knowledge. And so, in evolving a philosophy that took some of the most creative ideas of the "pagan" tradition, Christianity developed its doctrinal dimension in a powerful way. Christian philosophy supplied the framework for the emerging civilization of Christian Europe.

Every worldview now has an even more exciting and difficult task than that experienced by Christianity as it emerged in the Greek and Roman world. Today there are great shifts and advances in knowledge. Our cosmos has been greatly expanded. Christianity and other religions and worldviews are meeting one another in a new global dialogue. So each worldview has to come to terms with the values and insights of the others. Daunting—but out of it creative new thinking about human life may come.

The doctrinal dimension is also important because it may help to reflect and stimulate a fresh vision of the world. Buddhism, for instance, is strongly doctrinal in many ways, and tends to play down myth. It pays a lot of attention to the analysis of things and persons. It argues that everything we encounter in the cosmos is short-lived, that the things that we see as being enduring and solid—like mountains and monuments—are really clouds or swarms of short-lived processes. This is very much in tune with the picture of the material world presented by modern physics. Solid things are made up of atoms, which themselves are bundles of particles, and consist mostly of empty space. The Buddhist picture of the cosmos and of ourselves (for we too, according to the Buddha, are swarms of short-lived events) is not just a piece of theory; it is meant to make you look at the world in a new way, to recognize its "emptiness," and to see that there is nothing solidly satisfying to be had by our grasping for things. It is meant to give you an insight into the way we can gain liberation. So the doctrines have a practical meaning, not just a theoretical one. They provide a kind of vision or way of looking at things, which itself can inspire us to act, and guide our minds in a certain way.

It is almost inevitable that a religion, which develops doctrines, should be involved in philosophical thinking and debate. Already I have referred more than once to philosophy. Since this word has undergone various changes of meaning, it would be wise to reflect a little about what it means to us today.

It is, of course, a word of Western origin, and it reflects something of the ancient Greek world out of which it came. Other cultures do not have exactly the same concept; for instance, in India the term *darśana*, sometimes translated "philosophy" more literally means a viewpoint or worldview. It means more the *result* of philosophizing than the activity itself. The object of philosophy is to reflect broadly about human experience and knowledge in order to arrive at some overall conclusions about the world. But doesn't this view make philosophy the same as religion, for doesn't religion also end up presenting a view of the world? We ought to make three distinctions.

First, not all worldviews are religious. Some of them result from complex processes of reflection—from philosophy—rather than from the experiences or revealed myths at the heart of traditional religions. Second, the results of philosophy do not always add up to a system of belief that becomes embedded in a movement or institution. For instance, the ideas of German philosopher Immanuel Kant (1724–1804) are of great significance for all modern thinking in the West. But there is no separate religion or worldview called Kantianism. When we use this word we mean the structure of doctrines Kant evolved about such matters as the relation of science and ethics and of mathematics and perceptual experience. Philosophy provides not so much a total worldview as an important set of ingredients that can be used in expounding, amending, or defending a worldview. Third, in recent times philosophy has taken on a rather technical role. As studied by scholars and students, it tends to give a central place to logic and to a range of problems arising out of modern science. It has also been, in the English-speaking world, very concerned with the analysis of language. Thus in the West philosophy now tends to mean something rather narrower than in the past, when it often aspired to construct worldviews, to comment more directly on human values, and to serve as a framework for evaluating moral questions.

Because the term "philosophy" implies the act of reasoning—trying to reflect rationally about experience and human knowledge—there are sometimes currents of feeling in religious traditions that hold that philosophy is misleading or positively dangerous. Many think that the highest truth is not discovered by reason, but by revelation. This debate has a special relevance to the question of whether it is possible to prove there is a God. I shall return to this later on.

Aristotle remarked that you have to think philosophically because the question of whether you should or not is itself a philosophical question. If you conclude that religion is not a matter of reason, you have already been engaged in philosophy.

Not surprisingly, a general area of thinking called "the philosophy of religion" has evolved. It is concerned with reflections about how far reason can go in trying to arrive at religious truth. It can also, in a broader way, follow the logic of my argument in this book, and take in secular as well as religious worldviews. As such it becomes what may be called "the philosophy of worldviews."

Here, however, we get directly entangled in judgments about whether a given belief is true or false. We have crossed the line from description into the realm of evaluation. But first we must try to understand the structure of doctrines. Already we have done something in this direction by trying to see their various functions. I have already mentioned four. One is the function of bringing order into the material presented by tradition in the form of myth and religious experience. Another is to make clear the way in which religious symbols refer beyond themselves to what is ultimate and universal. A third is to relate the tradition to changes in knowledge. A fourth is to stimulate a vision of the world.

A fifth function, which has been of great importance especially in the West, is to define the community. Those who belong to the community have to accept a set of doctrines, and anything outside these may turn out to be heresy and warrant the expulsion of those who propound those ideas. This defining function of doctrines is less well marked in modern times, except in Marxist countries and in some parts of the Islamic world, because in Western countries greater individual freedom of choice in religion has made it impractical to insist on rules of orthodoxy. Still, in each tradition there is some scheme of belief that is typically accepted by its members, and such a system gives shape to the world as perceived by the group. In this sense there remains a definitional role that doctrine plays, but we should note that it plays it in conjunction with other dimensions of religion such as the style of ritual, and the mode of organization of the group. The doctrinal scheme is, in the case of Christianity, summed up in the Creed, an affirmation of belief in certain things, events, and ideas which together define the Christian's faith. In other words, when the Christian recites the Creed he is not just repeating what he believes but is subscribing to beliefs that define him as an orthodox member of the community. For what, after all, is the community but the body of people who affirm these things? Public affirmation is in itself an act in which the person reexpresses solidarity with the rest of the community.

This is one reason why fierce controversy and persecution have often sprung up over doctrines. If, in order to be saved, membership in the community is necessary or at least highly desirable (for it is through the community that the Christian is in solidarity with the savior), and if faith defines the community and is summarized in doctrine, then the community must be clear as to what is true doctrine and what is not. Those who deny true doctrine come to be seen as threats to the community and to the assurance of salvation. They are seen as subversive. It is easy in such a case to think that the Church is justified in persecuting them. There is, of course, an underlying question: How do we—how does anyone—know what the true doctrine is? We shall come back to this, as I have already said. But there is something more to be said in trying to understand how doctrines work.

More than once I have used the phrase "doctrinal scheme" to indicate that a religion or secular movement typically has a set of doctrines that are, so to speak, woven into a scheme. I have not used the word "system" here, as it is too rigid. The fact is that religious doctrines are not quite as systematic, say, as Euclid's geometry. You cannot begin from a few religious axioms and definitions and deduce the rest of the system. Indeed, rarely can you talk about proof. You can rarely say that one doctrine actually entails another; that is, you can only rarely say that believing one doctrine means that you absolutely *must* believe another, because the latter necessarily follows from the first one. Sometimes religious people think that it is part of the meaning or concept of "God" that he is good; so "X is God" would entail "X is good." But even here I have doubts for two main reasons. First, it by no means follows that because X created the cosmos X is good (a creator might be malicious, or neither good nor bad, or beyond good and bad). If we spell out more fully what we mean by God, calling him "creator of the cosmos," it still does not follow that God is good. Second, when we say that God is good we may not mean "good" the way we mean it when we say a *person* is good. In order to understand what is meant we may have to spell out the whole context in which God operates. So we can't, simply by looking at the words themselves, be sure what we mean in saying that God is good.

All this is a roundabout way of coming to the point that the pictures doctrines paint are not rigidly systematic. They incorporate many pieces that are put together like a collage. They are more like schemes than systems.

It is the task of the intellectual in a religious movement—the theologian, in the Western tradition—to try to get as much "system" into the scheme as possible, and to present it all in an orderly fashion. This way the faith becomes more clearly articulated. But there is always quite a lot of flexibility—a certain degree of looseness—about the way doctrines fit together.

In spite of this looseness, doctrines affect one another. They influence each other's meaning. Thus the nature of God in the Christian tradition differs from the nature of God in the Jewish tradition, because for Christians God the creator is seen in light of the doctrine that Christ is God. Thus at the start of St. John's Gospel there is a novel way of putting the creation story: "In the beginning was the Word, and the Word was with God. . . ." The passage goes on to identify the Word with Christ. Christ, though divine, is also human, and this human came into the world that in some sense he himself had created (but the world did not recognize its creator). This gives a whole new slant on the nature and purpose of God. So we can say that one major element in a scheme affects the other elements. A scheme is organic, a kind of loose organism, and to understand a scheme, it is important to see each part in the context of the whole. We can make a comparison with games. Every game has a scheme of rules. A goal in soccer differs from a goal in hockey, with each game having its own rules for scoring.

We might call this contextual element, then, the "organic" character of doctrinal schemes. Each scheme is unique. Christianity is unique because it has a scheme with a special shape, in part because the doctrines reflect the very particular mythic story of Jesus Christ. But Judaism is unique in a different way, for its scheme does not include doctrines about Jesus Christ, and evaluates the law quite differently. Although the two religions overlap and are alike in certain ways they each have their own special shapes.

While we can look at doctrines horizontally, so to speak, by seeing each in its own particular context, we can also consider them "vertically." That is, we can see how doctrines relate to other religious dimensions—experience and ritual, for example.

Let us illustrate this first by showing how the doctrine of God's omnipresence relates to experience and worship. "Omnipresence" is of course only a rather cumbersome expression for "being everywhere." According to classical ideas of God as creator of the cosmos, he is not just one who sets things in motion "in the beginning." Maybe (if Hindus are right) there is no beginning at all, only a cosmos in continuous change. God then becomes the continuous changer behind all the change—as though the cosmos is a tune and God the violinist who has always been playing. But whether or not we say the cosmos has a beginning, God is still "keeping things going." Thus he lies behind all the events that occur in the world. If the sun rises in the morning, then God is behind that. If the flower grows, then God is behind that. If the hail falls or the thunder growls, then God is behind that. If fire burns and flies bite, then God is behind that too. This, by the way, naturally poses what has been called "the problem of evil," for if bad and hurtful things happen, then God is behind them. How then can he be perfectly good? Maybe—and this is one way of trying to deal with the problem—bad things are the product of free human choices, like willful murders and cruelty. But there are bad and hurtful things caused naturally, by earthquakes and rabid dogs and viruses and storms at sea. Leaving this famous problem of evil to one side, the doctrine that God is present everywhere connects with the idea that he is "behind" everything that happens. His hand is everywhere—to use a metaphor (literally, of course, he has no hands).

I put "behind" in quotes above for good reason. It is not that God is quite literally *behind* what I see in front of me. I see a mountain from where I am writing this, but God is not the other side of the mountain (Milan, Italy, as it happens, is the other side of the mountain). God may be behind the wisteria leaves I see moving lightly in the breeze, but he is not literally behind them; an iron railing is literally behind them. So what does "behind" mean? It means that God exists in another, different dimension, energizing the cosmos. Maybe it is like me and my body. For I am, so to speak, "present" in my fingers: They respond to my directions and do what I want them to do. But you don't find me by cutting up my fingers and looking inside. God is working, as it were, within all things, but you don't find him by cutting them up and looking inside.

This doctrine that God as creative spirit is present within and behind all things has a strong significance in the dimension of experience. This is so in two ways. First, the doctrine means that the person with faith in God is always aware of God's presence: God is a friend and sustainer, and can always be turned to because he is never at any distance. His hand is seen in everything that happens. So a person of faith will have a strong sense of providence, of God's guidance over events. Even the bad things that happen may, in the long run, be good. Second, the idea that God is everywhere present corresponds to certain numinous experiences, when I may have a strong sense of God's powerful presence, or when, in the "panenhenic" feeling, I have a sense of communion with an unseen spirit pervading all that surrounds me.

So God is close by, and God surrounds me; but there is another way to explain my experience of him. The image that he is "behind" everything suggests a dualism; me here, God over there. This dualism derives from, and expresses, the spirit of the numinous and the sense of the "Wholly Other."

This is where the doctrine of God's omnipresence is relevant to ritual, too: to worship and prayer. For God can be worshiped anywhere if God is present everywhere. God may seem "more present" in some places and times (say, at the Eucharist or Mass, according to Catholics) than at others. But he is present everywhere and so can be everywhere contacted in worship and through prayer. There is no place where you cannot talk to God or feel his presence. These are the implications, at any rate, of the Christian and other monotheistic doctrines of creation.

So the doctrines of omnipresence and creation are not to be seen just as statements about how God relates to the cosmos. They are also beliefs that are real in experience and in the practical life of religion. For those who have faith they are living, vibrant ideas, not just theories. Let us now see how a rather different doctrine, that of the Void in the Buddhist tradition, works both in context and in relation to other dimensions.

Buddhist Doctrines

The division of Buddhist thought into Greater Vehicle Buddhism (Mahāyāna) and Lesser Vehicle Buddhism (of which Theravada is the predominant school) was largely due to differing interpretations of Buddha's teachings on attaining nirvana. Lesser Vehicle Buddhism emphasized self-discipline and individual achievement. Greater Vehicle Buddhism developed the idea of becoming a Bodhisattva—one who concentrates on ridding the suffering of others—and a new interpretation of the nature of the ultimate goal.

The doctrine I would like to discuss here—the doctrine that everything is śūnya, or empty, or void—arose in Greater Vehicle Buddhism. This doctrine is a reaction against the more traditional idea of nirvana found in Lesser Vehicle, and in particular Theravada, Buddhism. This school saw nirvana as liberation from the cycle of rebirth. It made a strong distinction between this world (that is, life in the cosmos and the cycle of rebirth, or saṁsāra) on the one hand, and the liberated state of nirvana on the other. Being a monk or nun is the bridge toward nirvana. You need to withdraw from the world to have a real chance of liberation. From the Greater Vehicle point of view there was too rigid a contrast between the monastic community and the ordinary people, or laity. Also, it was easy to think of the pursuit of nirvana as selfish—a higher selfishness, maybe, but still selfishness. Is the monk who seeks liberation not just looking after his own higher interests and trying thus to avoid future suffering? How does this square with the Buddha's continuous emphasis on being selfless and having compassion for other living beings?

The doctrine of the Void ingeniously and illuminatingly dealt with all these questions. It begins from the premise that everything is impermanent. What we take to be fairly solid is just a swarm of events (as we have already seen). One event follows from a package of other events, each of which depends on a package of prior events. Nothing has its own independence. More than this, even the idea that an event is caused by a package of others is at best a provisional sketch. Reflection will show that the idea contains problems, indeed contradictions. If everything is truly impermanent, each event is instantaneous. So by the time an event occurs the package of events giving rise to it will have vanished. How can that which now does not exist cause anything to happen? Even the idea that everything depends on something else is just provisional; at a deeper level it is without substance. The world of causal relationships is empty. So nothing we see has any genuine reality. The world is, at bottom, empty. The bottom line is zero, as we might say.

But at the same time the Greater Vehicle does not throw away the Lesser Vehicle's stress on meditation. The purification of consciousness is still the central element of Buddhist practice. Such an inner state, bringing one toward liberation, is one of higher emptiness, beyond thoughts and images. In realizing complete freedom from the events and packages that make up the cosmos one experiences one's inner nature—one's Emptiness. So by a strange paradox the realm of nirvana or liberation is the same as that of *saṁsāra:* The emptiness of liberation is the same as the emptiness lying at the heart of the cosmos and at its every process. The real nature of things is empty; the true nature of liberation is empty. Consequently, one does not have to leave the world in order to gain the higher truth.

There is another consequence. The Empty, in addition to being the true nature of nirvana, and the cosmos, is also the true nature of Buddhahood. The Buddha achieved a mystical experience of the ultimate. It was a non-dual experience. The ultimate is Emptiness itself. The Buddha achieved a non-dual state of unity therefore with the Empty. He became the Empty. Emptiness is the essential nature of the Buddha. In aspiring, therefore, to achieve a similar non-dual experience of the Empty, I myself aspire to become a Buddha. In non-dual Emptiness there are no distinctions—we are all, so to speak, the Buddha. This idea that we all can gain Buddhahood was put in a picturesque way in the Greater Vehicle when it was said that Buddhas are as numerous as the grains of sand along the river Ganges. One who is destined to become a Buddha is called a Bodhisattva; in the Buddhist tradition the Bodhisattva is one who sacrifices himself out of compassion for other living beings. Many stories of Guatama in a previous life testify to this idea: how as a hare he throws himself on a fire so that a hungry man should have food, for instance (folktales and the like were turned to good effect to illustrate the need for compassion). So the Greater Vehicle underlined the ideal of the Bodhisattva who, in his search for the ultimate, always turns aside to help others. Living in this world, he helps to spread the knowledge that at bottom liberation lies here—for Emptiness lies at the heart of everything around us, and in our selves.

Another term that is used is *Suchness*: The ultimate cannot be put into words, but only pointed at, as a finger points at the moon. The very word "Suchness" is meant to be like a finger. It points to what cannot be put into words. Here the doctrinal dimension shows how religious—and in particular, mystical—experience cannot be articulated in ordinary everyday language. Thus, a lot of philosophical thinking in the Greater Vehicle tries to illustrate the inadequacy of ordinary language by showing that all theories are true only at a surface level. At a deeper level truth is not to be spelled out—it is merely to be pointed to and experienced.

In short, the doctrinal dimension in this case ties in with the non-dual mystical experience and with the ethical demands of Buddhist compassion. The doctrines are a matter of experience and action as well as philosophy. Philosophy in this way becomes applied.

Whether we look East to Buddhist philosophy or West to reflection about God, there is great preoccupation with the nature of language. The Buddhist finds language misleading, for it assumes, wrongly, a solidity in the world, and assumes too that we have real selves—when the truth is that we too, seen in the light of the Buddha's insight, dissolve into swarms of events. We too are empty packages. For the Christian, Jewish, or Islamic theologian there is always the problem of how, or whether, the language used to talk about God really can be taken at face value. God is said to have hands, but does not. He is "behind," but not literally. And so theologians tend to come up with a theory of religious language—for instance, that everything we say positively about God has to be balanced by a negative, and that the only way we can speak of God is by *analogy*. According to this view, God is wise in a manner that fits with his nature, and perfectly, rather than in the way we are wise, which is relative to our nature, and imperfect.

Doctrines and Truth

So far we have been looking chiefly at the nature and function of doctrines. What about questions of whether or not they are true?

Traditionally in India there have been discussions about the sources of human knowledge, and usually three have been seen as most important, although not all schools of thought have accepted them all as valid. They are *perception, inference,* and *testimony*. For example: I know that there is smoke on the mountain I see because of *perception*. I reason that there is a fire on the mountain by *inference* (because I see smoke and make a deduction). If I heard on the radio that the fire had been started by an arsonist I would be accepting this information on *testimony*. The Indian tradition thought of religious experience as a kind of perception; for example, a mystic perceives the true nature of reality. Testimony was often thought of as being transcendental, that is, as having reference to that which lies "beyond" the cosmos. Thus, the Vedic scriptures were considered by orthodox Hindus to be testimony to the nature of the unseen divine reality. So we could recast the three sources as being *experience, reason* (which is the use of inferences), and *scripture*. In the West, too, there has been debate about the role of these three. For some, like Quakers, the most important source of spiritual truth is inner religious experience. For many evangelical Christians and for many Muslims the primary source of truth is scripture. For some thinkers it is possible to know that there is a Creator by reasoning (e.g., that the cosmos might not have existed, but does, so needs a Cause).

Traditionally in the West, this last idea has led to classifying knowledge of God under two headings—revealed theology and natural theology. "Natural" theology is knowledge that does not come through grace—that is, not through God's activity in revealing his will to us in the Scriptures and by revelation—but rather by the use of our natural endowments, in particular our reason. But it has been argued, chiefly by Protestant thinkers, that reason too is fallen. Because of the Fall humans can do not good without God (they argue), and this applies to all our natural capacities, including reason. Reason, being fallen, cannot give us knowledge of God.

At the same time, Kant and other more recent philosophers have criticized the traditional ways people have sought to "prove" God's existence. These traditional proofs found their classical form in the writing of Anselm (1033–1109), Aquinas (1224–1274), Descartes (1596–1650), and others. Basically they boil down to three main arguments.

The first, known as the Ontological Argument, was propounded by Anselm and Descartes and rejected by Aquinas. It gets its name from "ontology" (reasoned inquiry, *logy*, into *onto*, being). It basically argues that God is to be defined as the most perfect possible being. But in order to be perfect, a being *must* exist (and a being who does not exist is less perfect). So, given the definition, God as the most perfect being must exist. Only if he exists is he absolutely perfect. If he had all other perfections but lacked existence, then he would be missing one perfection—existence.

For various reasons many philosophers have rejected the validity of this argument. Chiefly they object to the idea that existence is a kind of perfection. They think of the verb "to exist" as telling you whether what you have in mind is out there in the real world, or just in your mind. In other words, "exists" functions in language and in logic in a different way from "is wise," "is good," and so on, which express qualities that may or may not be perfectly manifested in God. To say "tigers exist" is not to claim that tigers have some quality, but to say that the cosmos contains tigers.

The second main argument is the Cosmological Argument (concerned with reasoning about the cosmos). Basically it argues that since the cosmos does exist (and it might not have existed), it needs an explanation—a cause "lying outside" itself. Opinion about the validity of such a piece of reasoning is mixed. Some feel that it still has force: We can still ask for an explanation of the cosmos, once all the scientific evidence is in, about the scale of the cosmos and (maybe) the big bang, which exploded outward in early moments of the present cosmic era. Others think that we can only talk seriously and meaningfully about cause and effect within the realm of events inside the cosmos, within the sphere of what can be observed and measured. Go outside the cosmos and you can no longer talk meaningfully about cause and effect. For one thing, if I say *this* causes *that* I am talking in the framework of time, for the cause comes before the effect. But we have no concept of time out-side of the cosmos.

Already this argument raises an important issue about the relation of religion and science. Does religion have to be confined to what can be meaningfully dealt with by observation and measure-ment, and so by science? Much modern philosophy of religion has been concerned with this question. Is religious language (the lan-guage of myth, the language of mystical experience, the language of doctrines which point to the Beyond) the same as scientific lan-guage? Are there not different realms or levels of language, doing different things—science describing and explaining, religion expressing commitment and indicating meaning in life?

The belief that there are two realms of language, and that sci-ence and religion really have different roles and areas to which they apply, has two main forms. One is found in the existentialist writ-ers, and we have already alluded to one example of this in the thought of Rudolf Bultmann. For him science consists of "objective" inquiry. But there is also the realm of personal (subjective) relation-ships, and this is the realm of religion. The second main version of this belief goes back to the philosopher Ludwig Wittgenstein (1889–1951). He saw language as having multiple forms and uses, among them the function of depicting the world in ways that helped to mobilize feeling and action—and herein lies the realm of religion. Although he wrote mostly inside the Western cultural tradition, his viewpoint can be applied—as I attempted to show in *Reasons and Faiths* (1958)—in a crosscultural way.

There are, of course, those who reject the idea of "two realms." The positivists, particularly in the work of the English philosopher A. J. Ayer (b. 1910), regard talk of anything that lies beyond what can be perceived directly or indirectly as being meaningless. Sentences that purport to talk of God are without meaning, for they can have no cash value in perception. For example, if I say there is life in other galaxies (even though none can now be observed), my statement is a meaningful claim, because I can imagine ways in which one could, through ordinary perception, find evidence to sup-port it. We might, for instance, see evidence of it in some new mea-surements gained through observation by telescopes put into orbit around the earth. But if I talk of God, can there ever be any tele-scope that will reach him? The positivists, as their name hints, wish to stick to what *positively* can be found in science. No knowledge, they say, lies outside the scope of present or future science.

Marxists, too, if they are true to Marx's thought, reject religion not so much because it is meaningless, but because it is false.

Again they see everything falling within the realm of science (as they define it). There is nothing beyond this world.

But aren't these views in their own way dogmatic? Why should there not be two realms? And why shouldn't we follow the Indian writers and treat religious experience as a form of perception, and thus a valid source of knowledge?

The Cosmological Argument is important not because we think it proves anything, but because it raises the question of whether there is something beyond the cosmos.

The third main traditional argument is the so-called Teleological Argument (from *teleo*, that which concerns the purposive). It typically argues that the things or processes in the cosmos display design or purpose. The planets go around the sun in an orderly manner, rather like the parts of a machine, and animals' eyes are well adapted to the tasks required. So there must be a Designer. On the whole modern opinion denies the validity of this argument. One reason is that scientific theory has shown how to explain astronomy, and animal adaptation without going back to the idea of a Designer. Another reason this idea has lost favor is that there is a lot of disorder in the cosmos too. The cosmos is not, after all, very much like a machine. If we find a wristwatch on the beach we can infer the existence of an intelligent being who made the watch. But can we do the same with a sea shell and a piece of slime?

It may be that the best the old arguments do is not to prove God's existence, but to raise the possibility of it. But even here we meet with a further question. Why talk only in terms of the Western God? What about Buddhist Emptiness or the Tao of Taoism? There are many alternative religious traditions in this world to consider.

The existence of different religious traditions raises an issue about revelation or testimony as a source of knowledge. After all, many Christians or Hindus or Muslims may say that it does not matter about the traditional arguments; what is important is revelation (Bible, Veda, and Qur'ān). Yet the conflicts among the scriptures themselves lead us to ask questions. For example, how do we know one book of revelation is true rather than another?

In recent times particularly, we have been led to ask some vital new questions about the relationship of the great faiths. Why follow one rather than any of the others? So a new branch of the philosophy of religion may be called the "philosophy of religions" in the plural, or more broadly the "philosophy of worldviews." It would deal with the nature of religious truth and concepts in a crosscultural way.

In this context we are moved to think about religious experience as a source of knowledge of what lies Beyond. If we ask why we should take the Veda seriously, one main answer is, "These works are founded ultimately on the visions of early seers and sages." If we ask about the Bible, leaving aside its historical narratives, we might say, "Its ideas are founded on the visions of the great prophets and on the experiences of the risen Christ." If we ask about the Qur'ān, we are led to the revelatory experiences of the Prophet Muhammad. If we look toward Buddhism, at the heart of its message lies the enlightenment of the Buddha. So in all these cases we appeal to religious experience, and especially that of the great persons of faith, as the basis for our commitment to their way of seeing the world.

It is possible here to open up only briefly these deeper questions of philosophy. But we can sketch two positions, one skeptical of religion, the other positive. The second is (roughly) my own view.

The first is this: Modern folk can do without religion. There is no sense in speaking of a Beyond, for our only access to it would be by revelation of religious experience. But knowledge does not rest on old books; science advances and revises all that we once thought we knew. As for religious experiences, skeptics would move that those who have them—prophets and mystics—often conflict and this fact throws doubt on their validity. Skeptics also hold that we can explain religious experiences as the product of illusions born of our wish to find meaning outside of ourselves. They contend that it is better to change the world to alleviate suffering and improve human existence than to waste effort on dreaming of heaven. We need a secular worldview, not a traditional one.

The second position is this: Why is there a cosmos? What is the inner nature of things? We seem always to be driven by our questions beyond the realm of pure science. And similarly with our pursuit of worldly goals. Should we alleviate suffering and increase happiness? Of course, if we can, but what is true happiness, and what is the deeper nature of suffering? Religions contain spiritual experiences and symbols that give us a deeper view of these questions. We can see patterns of religious experience that suggest there are different models of the Ultimate as beyond the cosmos and yet somehow deep within our own consciousness. This is not surprising, since the whole of our experience revolves around the mystery of blind and mute nature evolving into conscious beings like ourselves, so that nature's colors and shapes themselves are in part a product of our consciousness. She makes us and we make her. Religion can throw light on this mysterious middle role of consciousness in our cosmos.

All this leads to the question, Which religion? One test, in my view, is whether a religion can make some constructive sense of other faiths; dismissing them as false and idolatrous is not making sense of them. Another test is whether a faith can live in harmony and creative interaction with science, and that means that, like science, it has to be critical of itself. In light of such tests, it seems to me that some phases of religion are better than others. I leave it, though, to you to pursue this line of exploration; for in our world, ultimately it is for me to decide for myself and you for yourself. And this also limits (I think) the authority of tradition. Even if I accept authority from outside of myself, it is I and no one else who does this. So the drift of reasoning about religion is toward you and toward your reflections and decisions.

Whatever we say about the truth of religion and personal decisions about it, the importance of doctrines as a dimension of human worldviews cannot be denied. Doctrines are organically related, as we have seen, to other dimensions of religion, among them ritual, through which we mobilize feelings and act out our symbols. Doctrines are also closely related to the value judgments we make, and among these are the moral values we bring to bear on life. We have noted that there is a question of what true happiness is, and the answer depends upon our view of the world. The question of happiness is closely related to moral action, much of which is concerned with trying to seek the welfare and happiness of others. This leads us into the realm of ethics, in a cosmic as well as a personal context. To that let us now turn.

Chapter
6

The Ethical Dimension

The ethical dimension of a religion or worldview is shaped by the other dimensions, but *it* also helps to shape *them*. If the numinous experience revealed to early Israel and to the prophets a mysterious and dynamic deity, their moral insights suggested that this God was a good God. He demanded not just sacrifices but also contrition, not just observance of the Sabbath but also uprightness in conduct. If the mystical experience revealed to early Buddhism a realm of peace and pure consciousness, moral insight also showed that this peace was to be shared with others, and that ultimately no inner illumination not accompanied by compassion for the suffering of other living beings was worth having.

Buddhists, Hindus, and Jains have a special attitude toward moral action because they believe in reincarnation. Since one may be reborn in animal or insect form, one must have a sense of solidarity with other living beings. In the religions of the West, however, the dominant view has been that human beings have souls but animals do not. In theory, at any rate, there is a greater moral obligation felt in their Indian traditions toward animals and other living forms than has been the case in the West. But in recent times in the West a greater concern with our living environment, together with the influence of the East on our culture, has led to changes in attitudes.We see campaigns to save whales and leopards, for example. Whatever our specific attitudes, there is no doubt that the scope of morality is affected by our general worldview.

Morality is affected also by our picture of the ideal human being. The Christian looks to Christ and to the saints and heroes of the tradition. The Buddhist looks to the Buddha, the Muslim to Muhammad, the Hindu to Rāma and Krishna and others, the Taoist to Lao-tse, and the Confucianist to Confucius.

So we can already see that there are ways in which the ethical dimension relates to religious experience, to doctrines about the cosmos and to the myth and historical heroes of the traditions.

In modern times an attempt has been made to try in one way or another to set up ethics on an independent basis—that is, independent of traditional religious belief. But as we shall see such an attempt cannot be completely successful, because every ethical system seems to raise questions about the worldview behind it.

Thus, probably the most powerful and influential ethical system—or set of systems—in modern times has been utilitarianism, which had it chief expression in the nineteenth century through the writings of John Stuart Mill (1806–1873). Its importance lies in trying to see moral action in terms of its utility, and utility in terms of whether something helps to produce human happiness or to reduce human suffering. It thus shapes much of modern politics and economics in the democratic West. In the West we tend to think in utilitarian terms: to think of whether a given aspect of our institutions, such as divorce law, will bring the greatest happiness to the greatest number and the least suffering to the least number. We conduct economic policy on the basis that we should prosper—in such a way so that everyone can realize a reasonable degree of happiness and freedom from poverty. The American constitution speaks of the pursuit of happiness, and socialism is often based on the idea that it will banish poverty and free people for better things. In such ways our whole Western culture is drenched with utilitarian thoughts.

This utilitarianism is often coupled with the idea, celebrated by the scientific humanist, that the basis of all values in the individual human being, and that what is most important is how individuals relate to one another. In his book *I and Thou*, the Jewish writer Martin Buber looks, as we have seen, to the deeper human relationships as the center of the meaning of life.

Somewhat opposed to the individualism of much of the West's thinking is the collectivism of the Marxist tradition. Here human behavior and economics are so closely woven together that ethics is also seen as collective: Actions are good insofar as they bring about a revolution that will consolidate socialism, or insofar as they preserve the revolution and help in the march toward an ideal society in which human beings live in harmony.

Either the study of religious ethics can deal with the facts about morality and structures of moral thinking, or else it can reflect on what is right and wrong from a normative stance. Our prime concern here is with the former approach, but I shall say something briefly about the normative questions in due course; that is, about what ethical values we might adopt.

Comparative Religious Ethics

The crosscultural study of religious ethics is sometimes called "comparative religious ethics." This is quite a recent coinage, and only in the last few years has a really systematic attempt been made to open up the field. However, there were some notable previous enterprises that dealt with ethics in a comparative way. Perhaps most important among these was the *Encyclopedia of Religion and Ethics*, edited by James Hastings before, during, and just after World War I. The *Encyclopedia*, in many enormous volumes, gave liberal and learned treatment to a host of vital themes in the study of religion and, as its title implies, included much on moral views and practices everywhere in the world.

At one level, comparative religious ethics is aimed simply at delineating the various moral systems found in societies all over the world. Sometimes it is necessary to distinguish between what are called the great and the little traditions. For instance, one can view the ethical beliefs of the Sri Lankans from the angle of the great tradition, namely, official Buddhist belief as expressed through the scriptures and the preaching of the monks. But one can also see what the actual beliefs are in the villages of the highlands (for example), where elements other than "official Buddhism" come into play. Or, one could look to what the actual moral outlook is, say, of the average Italian as compared with the official teachings of the Catholic Church. Probably it is enough for us to say that just as there are many Buddhisms and many Christianities, so there are many Buddhist moralities and many Christian moralities.

When we find that there are in fact, likenesses and differences among cultures in regard to right and wrong, we begin to ask wider questions. What accounts for these likenesses and differences? One thing we might begin to do is to correlate moral values with kinds of doctrines, myths, and experiences.

But the major faiths have much in common as far as moral conduct goes. Not to steal, not to lie, not to kill, not to have certain kinds of sexual relations—such prescriptions are found across the world because such rules are necessary if there is to be a society at all. The widespread breaking of these rules would lead to chaos. Society can exist only where such wrong acts are in the minority.

However, what they mean in greater detail may vary quite a lot. In matters of sex, for example, there are varying systems. The Christian generally has only one wife, divorce notwithstanding—and for a long time in much of the Christian tradition even divorce was ruled out. The Muslim male, in contrast, may have up to four wives at one time, and divorce is built into the original legal system. As for killing, some societies allow the right of self-defense, and in war the killing of the enemy may be deemed a duty. Some religions are cautious about war or exclude it altogether, as do the Quakers; for others war is a natural means of spreading the domain in which the faith is exercised. This is notably so in the Islamic idea of the *jihād*, or holy struggle.

The way in which the rules themselves are viewed often differs, and this means that there are different models of virtue. For the Jew and the Muslim, for instance, the rules are part of the fabric of divinely instituted law—Torah and Shari'a, respectively. Obedience to the rules is obedience to God. In Judaism, obedience is qualified by the belief that the commandments are part of a contract or covenant between God and his people. In Buddhism the rules of morality are part of the "eightfold path" that leads to ultimate liberation. It is not that God has to be obeyed, but rather that, as part of the general effort at self-purification, it is wise to be good. The model for the monotheist is the obedient person of faith, such as Abraham. The model Buddhist is the person of superior insight.

Although Hinduism often involves belief in one divine Being, it shares with Buddhism a sense that the law or dharma is not so much something that is commanded by God, but rather that it is part of the nature of the world. The law is part of the fabric of the cosmos, so that to follow it is to follow the natural bent of things. Thus Hinduism makes the caste system (itself controlled by dharma) an aspect of cosmic order. Moreover, the order of the world includes the way the moral fabric of things is expressed through karma. My moral acts will bear fruits both in this life and in subsequent existences. So even if ultimately—as some believe—karma is controlled by God, there is still a natural mechanism that rewards good and punishes evil. This comes to be tied in with the idea of merit: The wise person acquires merit through his or her good deeds so that he or she may be reborn in more propitious circumstances.

In order to see in more detail how belief and spiritual practice affect ethics, it may be useful to sketch the dynamics of a number of systems.

I have already alluded to the way in which in the Buddhism of the Theravada, ethical conduct is woven into the eightfold path and so becomes part of the means of attaining liberation. This helps to explain why one of the five precepts of Buddhism forbids taking "drugs and intoxicants" (the word covers liquor and other things) because liquor clouds the mind and also arouses anger. The clouding of the mind must be avoided because the task of the saintly person is to cultivate clarity of consciousness and self-awareness. It is through this clarity that detached insight can be gained; such insight is liberating and can bring about ultimate decease and escape from the round of rebirth. Further, anger and allied emotions are the opposite of the peace that liberation should bring. So far, then, we can see the ban on drugs and liquor as fitting into the way a person should train herself. But not everyone is at all close to gaining nirvana. Monks and nuns are sometimes thought to be closer to attaining nirvana, but the ordinary lay people may have their chance in some future life. The teaching of karma and rebirth binds together the differing layers of Buddhist society by projecting a person's career into the future beyond the grave. The ordinary person gains merit by virtuous acts in this life and hopes for some better state in the next. Indeed, the person who gives generously to the Order and follows the moral path may be reborn in a heaven. This heaven, though, is not everlasting. It is not the final goal. Here is a major difference between Buddhism and traditional Christianity. In Christianity the final judgment consigns people to heaven or hell. But in Buddhism, a person's merit is in due course exhausted, and she is obliged to disappear from paradise and be reborn in some other state—perhaps as a nun close to gaining nirvana. This is in accord with the Buddhist idea that all existence, including heavenly (and for that matter hellish) existence, is impermanent: Only nirvana is the Permanent, and it lies beyond existence, beyond this world and the next.

In brief, Theravada Buddhism has traditionally seen morality as part of the path that leads to nirvana, and as something that operates within a universe controlled by karma. Karma is the law of reward and penalty within the framework of rebirth, in which my status as human or animal or whatever results from my acts in previous lives. In Theravada Buddhism, morality is seen as partly a matter of being prudent—either because it helps achieve the state of final freedom and true happiness, or because at least it helps to give you a better life next time around. Morality also involves peace and, in some degree, withdrawal from the bustle of the world. This Buddhist moral code has two tiers: There is a higher, more severe, level of personal conduct for monks and nuns, a less rigorous ethic for the laity and the mass of the people.

The ethic of Islam, in contrast, has quite a different atmosphere. For one thing, it does not (until we get to the mystical movement of inner quest known as Sufism) have two levels. It is a religion that applies equally to all men under Allah. The duality between the numinous Allah and his humble worshipers gives the latter a sense of equality and humility. Thus, in Islam (the word literally means "submission to God"), there is a strong sense of brotherhood. It is true that, from a modern Western point of view, there is inequality for women. Islamic law and custom, stemming from the Qur'ān and from the developing tradition, impose restrictions on women. Men can have up to four wives at once, but polyandry (that is, a woman having several husbands) is ruled out. Although it is not laid down in revelation, the custom of wearing the veil is widespread for women in Muslim countries. Even if women have property rights, and are protected by what in the time of the Prophet was essentially a reforming movement, some might think women's status inferior. But this is not the way orthodox Muslims view things. For them, Islamic law treats women and men as being separate and equal, because they have separate natures and functions.

The Otherness of Allah, which flows from the numinous character of the Prophet's revelations, means that all that is created is seen as coming from him; the laws by which people are supposed to live flow from him too. Thus the pattern of religious experience that was so central in the rise of Islam is consistent with, and indeed favors, the belief that there is a divinely instituted law. It happened also that early Islam saw itself as related to other revelations: So, too, in Islam there was Law, but Law with its own special features, for this was a new revelation to Muhammad that would set its seal upon the other traditions.

The emphasis on law also sprang from the strong sense of community in early Islam. Not only are all men under Allah brothers, but there is a particular community that has his blessing. The community was brought into being under the leadership of the Prophet, and before his death had succeeded in uniting a large part of the Arabs of his immediate region. The Islamic community was just embarking on those spectacular victories which stretched the new imperial power from Afghanistan to Morocco and from Spain to Iran. So the Law became the way the details of community life were defined. It covers much more than morals in the narrow sense: It embraces questions of finance, slavery, ritual, and so on.

Along with their moral teachings, religions tend to demand certain religious duties, such as keeping the Sabbath, going on pilgrimage, giving alms to the monastic order, and so on. They are religious duties rather than ethical ones in the sense that the latter directly concern people's dealings with other people. Religious duties deal especially with duties to God or duties to those who in some special way manifest religious truth. The idea behind such duties is often that they simply arise from the nature of faith: The person who loves God worships him, and this is a religious duty as well as being a result of such love. Sometimes they are seen as duties because they help to bring about that kind of feeling that makes them a joy as well as an obligation. Sometimes they can be seen as a kind of exchange: The Buddhist who gives food to monks or nuns gets from them teachings that help him or her on the path toward perfection.

The importance of brotherhood and the community in Islam is seen in the requirement to give alms. The poor brother or sister is helped. The duty when called on to fight a *jihād*, or holy war, on behalf of Islam reflects the fact that Islam does not make a sharp division between Church and State. The aim is to build a society that is Islamic, and this may mean using all the levers of power, including war, against the enemies of Islam. Since Allah is, in essence, power—however much Allah may also be compassionate and merciful—it is not surprising that earthly power should be seen as a way of expressing and strengthening Allah's dominion. By contrast, Buddhism centers not on power but peace, even emptiness, and tends to have an "otherworldly" outlook. The problem of Buddhist kingship is the issue of how power can be used at all, for power may mean trampling on the lives of people, thus corrupting our consciousness and storing up bad forces of karma.

The contrast between the Islamic and Buddhist traditions comes out also in the figures of the great founders. Muhammad was not just a man of God; he was the skillful diplomat, statesman, and general. The Buddha, according to predictions at his birth, was either to become a political world-conqueror or a spiritual one. In leaving his princely palace and setting out on the quest for truth through poverty and homelessness he gave up all worldly power. In return he gained enlightenment, and in fact helped to shape the world that came after him. But there he was—the lone sage, lean from fasts, his eyes unmoving beneath the tree as he attained purity of consciousness and that inner light that for him lit up the nature of all the world and became the source of his teaching. He was diplomatic in his preaching skills, and kingly in his noble demeanor. But he was not literally either a diplomat or a politician, still less a general. Three centuries or so afterward, the Indian emperor Ashoka destroyed a neighboring people in his pursuit of wider imperial power; but he was so tormented by his aggressive actions that henceforth he tried to rule as a king of peace. At the heart of Buddhism there is a dilemma about power.

Christianity presents a third face. (And Buddhism, too, evolved a somewhat different emphasis in its later forms.) Christianity's face is that of Christ's, and he unites in himself motifs that help to shape Christian ethics. Through much of Christian history Christ basically has come in two guises: as the God who, becoming human, met death upon the Cross, and as the God who, risen into the heavens, comes to judge the living and the dead, at the dreadful and glorious end of human history. The first Christ is empty of power, in the worldly sense; the second is the essence of majesty. The one is the suffering Servant, the other the fearful Judge. All of this reflects the fact that Christians have seen Christ as both human and divine. He lives in two worlds: In our earthly world he bears the marks of humility and love, and in the other, the numinous power which belongs to the divine Being.

To some extent this ambiguity is found in the way the New and Old Testaments relate to each other. Christianity inherited much of the early Jewish tradition, but looked at it in a different way. It kept some of the old Law, notably the Ten Commandments, but it thought that Christ himself was now the pattern for living, and so his life, death, and resurrection brought in a new covenant. Although Christians thought of the old covenant as part of the way God revealed himself to people—and to the people of Israel in particular—there was no need to follow the Law in the old way.

The two faces of Christ have given Christian morality a tendency toward inner struggle. Thus, for the early Church, participation in warfare was wrong, as Christians sought to live a harmless and upright life. Yet the Church was the extension of God's power and had responsibility to the world God had created. When the Church came to dominate the Roman Empire, emphasis began to be shifted to theory of the "just" war. A war might justly be fought in self-defense; later also religious wars, known as the Crusades, became duties. Christ as judge came to be seen as the embodiment of power in the service of justice.

But at the heart of Christian morality is the ideal of *agapē*, or reverential love: the love of God and neighbor. This love for other human beings extended to one's enemies, following the example of Christ, who had said "Father, forgive them" from his Cross. This reverential love stemmed partly from the perception that every person is made in the image of the Creator and thus in the image of Christ himself.

Christian views of ethics are also much affected by the doctrine of the Fall. Judaism has not made of Genesis what the Christian tradition has. For Christianity Adam's acts implicate the whole human race in a disaster, as a result of which human nature is corrupted. Humans are not able to be virtuous by themselves but need the help of God, through grace. The great emphasis on original sin arises from the conviction that Christ's death made a critical difference to the relationship between God and the human race. So it was clear that the greatness of Christ as "second Adam" must be reflected in the vast significance of the first Adam's act, whereby he and Eve and all of us became separated from God. The salvation in Christ presupposed the Adamic disaster. Thus, Christianity has seen human nature as being unable to perfect itself by human action—only by tapping the power or grace of Christ can the Christian grow in moral stature. A major thought of the early reformers, Luther in particular, was that the Roman Catholic Church suggested that people could (and should) improve their spiritual status by going on pilgrimages, giving to the Church and the poor, attending Mass, and so on. All of this suggested that people could gain something by performing good works, when it is only through God's grace (said Luther) that we can do anything good.

This position holds that much depends on the means of grace, that is, the way through which the Christian is supposed to receive the power of Christ. In much of mainstream Christianity, Catholic and Orthodox, that power comes primarily through the sacraments, above all the Mass or divine Liturgy. For much of later Protestantism, the chief sacrament is the Word—Christ as found in the Bible and in preaching, stirring people to holy living. The sacraments stress the divine side of Christ; preaching often brings out the human side. In the one case we receive power through the action of God in ritual; in the other case we gain power through inspiration and the example of the man Jesus.

Many of the later disputes about details of morality spring from some of these ideas and practices. The Catholic Church's defense of marriage as a lifelong union and its opposition to divorce owe a lot to the notion that marriage is a divinely created sacrament. The sacrament of marriage confers God's inner grace and power on a couple and a family through the physical and social acts of living together. The Christian debate with others over abortion stems from the question of the sanctity of human life, which in turn has to do with the doctrine that the individual is made in the image of God. And Christian social action, such as that of Mother Teresa of Calcutta, stems from this same sense of reverence for others, which is part of true love, following Jesus' example.

If Christian attitudes demonstrate a tension between this world and the other, so there is a tension in Buddhism between liberation and compassion. As we have seen, there is a certain prudence about right behavior: Being good helps toward the attainment of final release, or at least in getting a better life next time around. But compassion for the suffering of others should mean sacrificing oneself, even one's own welfare. Even nirvana may have to be put off if I am to serve my suffering fellow beings. Out of this self-sacrifice there came to be—as we have seen—a strong emphasis in Greater Vehicle Buddhism on the figure of the Bodhisattva, the being destined for Buddhahood who nevertheless puts off his own salvation in order to stay in the world to help others. There were various figures of Bodhisattvas who came to be revered and worshipped, such as the great Bodhisattva Avalokiteśvara who, as his name implies, "looks down" with compassion upon those who suffer in the world. The Bodhisattva was thought to have attained such a vast store of merit through his many lives of self-sacrifice (given that he had gained enough already to be "due" for nirvana) that he could distribute this immense surplus to others to help them on their way. Thus, the otherwise unworthy faithful person could, by calling on the Bodhisattva, gain extra merit, bringing him or her closer to final release from suffering. So in many ways the Greater Vehicle idea runs parallel to Christianity. But instead of the idea of love or *agapē*, in Buddhism compassion is central.

Just as in Christianity "living in the world," rather than withdrawal from the world, was emphasized, so in the Greater Vehicle the sharp cleft between nirvana over there (so to speak) and worldly life here, was called into question. It is possible for the Buddhist to pursue his ideal of imitating the Bodhisattva (indeed of *becoming* a Buddha-to-be) through living the good life in this world. Sometimes this had strange results. In medieval Japan the warrior class came to see techniques like archery and swordplay as methods which, if suitably adapted, could teach selflessness. In this manner even warfare would be a means of gaining higher insight. On the whole, however, Buddhist ethics have been eager to minimize violence.

The Nature of Morality

In all these examples we can see that ethics is not treated in isolation, and what is right and wrong is seen in the light of a wider cosmic vision. Yet in modern philosophy, especially since Kant in the late eighteenth century, there has been a quest to establish what Kant called the "autonomy," or independence, of morals. Philosophers have tried to show that right and wrong can be defined independently of some wider superstructure of belief. What is right and wrong is right and wrong not because God or the Buddha says so: God or the Buddha says so because he sees what is right and wrong. What is right is right because it is right on its own account, not because God says so. Kant thought the test of what is right and wrong is the so-called categorical imperative, to which he gave various formulations. In essence it amounted to a two-sided demand. One side holds that anything moral beings will must, to be right, be capable of being a universal law, that is, a law that all can follow. The other side holds that I should treat another human being always as an end in himself and never merely as a means. Kant thought these principles were categorical, not hypothetical. A categorical imperative is absolute; it applies unconditionally. A hypothetical imperative is, by contrast, one that applies only if some condition is met. For instance, the imperative, "If you want to avoid lung cancer, give up smoking" is hypothetical, because it depends on a condition, namely that you want to avoid lung cancer. You might not care. But (according to Kant), "Do not steal" is unconditional. It applies whatever your desires are. Indeed, typically, moral imperatives run contrary to what you want. A moral demand is one that I can will to become a universal law. Thus, stealing cannot become universal without a contradiction. If people did not refrain from stealing there would be, could be, no private property; without property there would be nothing to steal. Likewise it would be self-contradictory to imagine universal lying. If everyone lied there could be no orderly system of communication, and language would collapse. So the very use of language presupposes truth-telling.

Kant thought also that the categorical imperative as a test of what is right and wrong is not something imposed on the individual from outside. To act morally one has to revere the moral law and apply it to oneself. So each moral person is a legislator and, in a sense, the source of morality. It is presupposed that all people, as the source of morality, are to be given reverence. Hence the second formulation of the categorical imperative, requiring us to treat another person never merely as a means but also always as an end in herself. So treating a person, say a prostitute, merely as a means for producing pleasure, is an offense against the moral law.

All this implies that we can by reason establish what is right and wrong; morality does not have any external source, not even God. It derives, as I have said, from each person as his or her own moral legislator.

But although Kant argued for the independence of morality, and so was the forerunner of many other Western thinkers who believe that you can have "morals without religion," he thought that from a practical perspective God was presupposed by the moral law. It seems incongruous that virtue should not be matched by happiness. But in this world it is not possible for the virtuous person to gain the bliss that he or she deserves. Moreover, it is not even possible in our brief lives to achieve absolute goodness or moral perfection. We can only attain an approximation. Yet, in principle, the moral law makes absolute demands on us. Kant thought that the demands of the moral law in practice indicate that we should live on after death, and that God should in the end match our virtue with full happiness. So God and immortality are practical outcomes of the demands of the moral law. Although morality does not derive from God, we can infer a God from the moral law.

Instead of immortality, Kant could no doubt have thought of reincarnation as an alternative model of the upward striving for ultimate perfection. Had he been an Indian he might have come to very different conclusions about the presuppositions of the moral law, and karma might have taken the place of God. What appear to us as reasonable conclusions from within the perspective of our own culture may in fact look different from another cultural perspective.

There are other problems with Kant's position. Not all moral rules conform to his test. Although he may be right in thinking that stealing and lying contain, if universalized, an inner contradiction, this does not so obviously apply (for example) to incest. We could imagine a society that does not have a strict rule against incest. Perhaps it would not break down, although it might be inferior to ours. There are also problems with the exceptions that inevitably seem to have to be made to any rule. Wouldn't stealing bread to feed a starving child be justified if there were no other way to get food? Kant's doctrines have been subject to much debate. Refinements of his approach—what might be called the logical approach—to morality have been made in modern times. But partly because of difficulties in his position, many modern philosophers have looked to consequences as holding the key to right and wrong.

In this view, known as utilitarianism, the test of a rule or an institution or an action is whether it brings the greatest happiness to the greatest number of people and/or the least suffering to the least number. Stealing becomes wrong not only because it harms individuals, but also because it encourages people who militate against society. There are problems with the utilitarian view as well. What if sacrificing a small minority led to greater happiness for the majority? We might justify treating people merely as means if all we were interested in was worldwide happiness or suffering. Kill a person for some crime, in order to keep society orderly and make people safer and happier: Is this not treating the criminal just as a means? The next thing we know, we might treat noncriminals in the same way.

A Normative View

Already we are sliding into questions of what is normative. What is actually right or wrong? Up to now we have been trying to look at patterns of ethical thought in relation to the religious ideas and practices that shape them. What I now venture to say on what I think to be right and wrong is only one opinion (I have no special authority), and there can be many others. But it might be interesting for you to think about some of the ideas that occur to someone, like myself, who has immersed himself in the comparative study of religion and of comparative religious ethics.

The first thing to see is that we live in a global city in which different cultures and worldviews interact. When one group seeks to impose its standards on a group that does not share the same values, conflict arises. So it seems to me that there is a great case for religious toleration, and for a form of society in which there can be genuine plurality of beliefs and values. This toleration should breed an ethic of what might be called social personalism: I respect the social values of the other person because I respect the person in question—what another loves I love (in a way) because I love her.

But second, it seems to me that the purport of religion is to stress the spiritual life—worship of God, a vision of the goodness of the world, the practice of meditation, a perception of the impermanence of things, and so on. Morality has to be related to such spiritual vision and life. It is true that the religions do not agree by any means and their atmospheres often greatly differ. But they still are like fingers pointing at the moon; they point to what lies Beyond. This pointing to what lies beyond challenges the "worldly" notions of happiness and welfare that often enter into the calculations of modern folk, in the utilitarian tradition. True peace of spirit can (I would suggest, from a religious angle) be achieved only if one is in relationship to what lies Beyond. What is needed is *transcendental humanism*: prizing human welfare but seeing it in the light of a vision of what is eternal.

We can learn something from the tension in religion, between the dynamic power of the numinous experience and the tranquility of the mystical. There is a tension, too, between the divine and human sides of Christ, and between the otherworldly and this-worldly sides of insight and compassion in Buddhism. The religious person should not shrink from action in the world, and we should welcome the turbulence of human creativity and drive. But it has to have a balancing sense of peace. Thus it would seem to me that at times we cannot shrink from the use of force; society needs it to maintain order, and nations and classes may need protection from genocide and slavery. But the true aim should always be to minimize violence. As we sometimes cause pain to minimize pain, as in surgery, so we may use force to minimize violence. This attitude is often not reflected in the machismo of police forces or the nationalist hatreds of the military, although they often say that their true aim is order and peace. Force and violence are distasteful, and because they are minimally needed their excessive and common use should not be condoned.

Ultimately we need the sense of the Beyond in order to see anew the sacredness of the person. In a sense, each person is a world, a cosmos in itself. The world is alive when the cosmos and human consciousness interact, and the fields are lit up with green, the sky with blue, the birds with fluttering motion, the rain with wetness, and the sun with warmth. From my cosmos I should revere the world of others. Persons are in this way like gods, and should be treated with reverence in their creativity and joy, and with compassion in their lonely suffering. Religions give differing expressions to the overarching meaning attached to each individual. Faith helps us to see the immortal dignity of each person.

Well, religions have often used force on people and have often been intolerant. In our own day, secular worldviews have engaged in force and practiced intolerance of human values. But perhaps because of this, the religious and secular worldviews can learn from mutual criticism.

Chapter

7

The Ritual Dimension

In looking at the ethical dimension we have seen something of the values, and of the actions controlled by values, that enter into our lives. But equally central to religion, and vital for living worldviews, is the dimension of ritual. We may talk about belief in God as though it is just a matter of thinking that some statements are true—that a creator of the world exists, that he or she is good, and so on; but more deeply and more directly God is the being who is to be worshiped.

What is worship? Well, I can worship God in my heart and you cannot in any obvious way see what is going on. But it is also typical and somehow more basic for worship to take a partly outward form. Worshipers bow down, kneel, or stand up and sing. More elaborately they may pay their reverence to God or a god by making a sacrifice or going on a pilgrimage. Ritual is often assisted by various external visible means, such as the use of candles, flags, chapels, temples, statues, icons, and so on. Look at a cathedral and you are, so to speak, looking at an act of worship frozen into stone. Look at a crucifix and you are looking at a feeling of faith congealed into wood and metal. And music, that wonderful and wordless way of expressing feelings, can be audible adoration, a flow of sound dedicated to sacred things. So there is basically a strong outer aspect to ritual in general and to worship in particular. Typically ritual has a bodily basis, so that worship is a bodily reaction to something unseen.

We saw earlier that language is often used performatively. We do things with words, as when with "I promise" I promise, and with "Thanks" I thank. Performative acts also consist of bodily gestures, as when I agree by nodding, or I greet by smiling, or I mourn by weeping. In ritual both words and bodily gestures typically are used, and ritual acts thus are a special class of performative acts. They range from highly formal acts (or at least those given precise form), like the Mass in the Catholic tradition, to less formal and more flexible acts—for instance, personal prayer does not have any fixed form, and I could pray while walking along, kneeling, or sitting.

The importance of ritual in religion is like the importance of performative acts in social life. If I am walking along the street and see a friend, I wave. I do this out of friendship, so my act helps both to express my warm friendly feelings and to reinforce the bond between the other person and myself. It is an act of communication, but I am not communicating information. Rather I impart a feeling and reinforce a relationship. Religious ritual also conveys feelings and relationships, and indeed often transfers an unseen reality from one sphere to another. For instance, the Catholic Mass conveys something of Christ to the participant: The body and blood of Christ—his essence—are conveyed to the person taking communion. The bread and wine *become*, in the rite, one's body and blood, so there is a double transformation. The material things are first transformed, and in being consumed by the participant they enter into and change a person.

The modern study of religion has made much progress in analyzing and understanding the ritual process. Let us look at two examples, namely sacrifice and so-called rites of passage.

Rituals of Sacrifice

In one kind of sacrifice the firstborn of a flock is sacrificed to a god or to God. The logic of the operation is complex. First, the firstborn is the ideal representative of the flock: Being the first stands for the whole, and as we have seen we often celebrate the class or whole of something by celebrating the first (the first persons to fly, the first to stand on the moon, the first human being, etc.). Second, the rite of sacrifice involves making the victim sacred. This indeed is the literal meaning of the term in the Latin word *sacrificium* from which the English is derived. Why does the thing sacrificed have to be made sacred? Because it is to be transferred to the Beyond, to the sacred god; and sacredness attracts the sacred and repels the profane (what is not sacred). So if the sacrificial offering is, so to speak, to make the journey from the seen to the unseen world it must be "attractive" to the god. Thus, the ritual includes selecting a perfect specimen, if not the firstborn, and conferring purity on it. The specimen reflects the nature of the god who has an ideal, pure nature. But at the same time the god has power. For example, in ancient Greece people made sacrifices to Poseidon, the god of the sea (originally a god associated with horses—as if the Greeks graduated from wild chariots on the plains of their early native lands in southern Russia to the carriages of the sea). The idea was to be on good terms so that the god might be appeased, grateful for the solemn sacrifice. The god was an unseen Being whose face, as it were, was the sea and whose body was the ocean; whose facial expression could be stormy and whose frown was like a hurricane; whose smile could be limpid and sparkling; and whose laughter was the chuckling waves under the boat's prow.

Some have thought of sacrifice as a case of (to use a Latin phrase) *do ut des*: "I give in order that you will give." It seems almost as though religion here is a matter of bribery. But it is probably truer to most sacrifice to characterize it as *do et das*: "I give and you give," or, to spell it out a bit more, "I give to you and hope that you as a kind being, well-disposed toward me, will grant me what I want." So the sacrifice opens up communication with the god in a benign manner, establishing good relations.

When I give a present to a friend it is a concrete sign of my friendship; it is a gift between equals. If a true friend, she will doubtless reciprocate. But the relation of human and god is not equal, so the human being has to make his sacrifice into an act of praise. Praise or worship acknowledges the god's might as well as the inferiority of the worshiper. Greek myths are littered with stories of those who wrongly try to be equal to the gods and neglect such an acknowledgment of our lower nature. Disaster overtakes them for their *hybris* (as the Greek has it), their grasping pride, their undue ambitiousness. It is also said that those whom the gods love die young. The person of fortune and talent is like the gods, and as if in fear of such a person's rivalry the gods, jealously, cause his early death. There is a hint of this attitude in the story of Adam and Eve: Having eaten of the tree of the knowledge of good and evil they become like gods, threatening the creator. Such are mythic ways of indicating the gulf between the ideal and powerful beings of the Beyond, and us mortals. So, in brief, the sacrifice involves praise and the acknowledgment of divine superiority. A sacrifice occurs in the context of worship.

If we follow the logic of sacrifice further, we can ask why the sacrificial being is killed. And why is it sometimes burnt? The victim is killed because it is taken out of the visible world and sent to the unseen world. The essence of the being—its soul—migrates to the Beyond. Burning a sacrifice is a particularly meaningful transformation: It transforms the victim into sky-going smoke, and the essence of the sacrifice rises upward and disappears in the direction of the abode of the gods.

Incidentally, and to amplify what we have earlier noted, consider the symbolic web of ideas surrounding the very notion of *upward*. The gods are superior; but "superior" literally means "above" or "higher up," while "inferior" means "lower down." We talk of high quality, lofty ideals, promotion, a top executive, a towering personality, top-level decisions, and so on. Height symbolizes goodness, power, and perfection. Lowness symbolizes humility, powerlessness, poor quality. So in the mythic schemes of the cosmos there is glorious heaven above beyond the sky, purgatorial and gloomy regions below in the underworld, and the middle earth, the intermediate mixed realm where we have our life.

In short, the sacrifice, although it involves an unequal relationship, creates a path of communication between humans and the god. Because the human beings give what is theirs, they give "part" of themselves, and thus express their solidarity with the god.

The performance of sacrifices in the past was often aimed at influencing a god's behavior in some material way. It was thought that different parts and aspects of nature were controlled by divine forces, and were, so to speak, animated matter. The sea or the wind or the sky or a river or fire could be separate expressions of different gods. A god would relate to the material expression as a soul to a body. Sacrifices were like gifts that established good relations with such forces and aspects of nature. But sacrificial ritual could have a more obviously ethical and spiritual meaning. The sacrifices offered to Yahweh in the Temple at Jerusalem could be seen as ways of giving honor and dominion to the one God, or as being ways of expiating bad behavior and sin. This is natural enough, too, in human relations: The husband who "makes up" to his wife after a quarrel by bringing flowers is acting like a sacrificer, for the flowers, if accepted, create or recreate a bond, and the breach is healed.

The gods of mountain and stream and sun and fire have faded over much of the world, and the sacrifices of the God of Israel have long since been discontinued, however much their meaning may be pondered by modern students of the Torah. Sacrifice no longer has the power it once had. But the principles it exhibits are still vital, for sacrifice shows something about the essential transactions involved in human–God relationships. If blood sacrifices have faded, offerings of other sorts still are made, as ways of opening up communication with what lies Beyond.

At one time in the history of the modern study of religion there was great debate about the relation between religion and magic. The debate carries on to some degree among anthropologists. Doesn't sacrifice sometimes look rather like magic? Magical rituals, however, are those that use formulas and performative acts to influence events more or less independently of the gods—like sticking pins in a wax image to bring trouble and pain upon my enemy, or uttering an incantation as I sow a crop to ensure its fertility. Such uses of ritual techniques have often been entangled in religion. Very often they are a testimony to our "trying anything." In matters where we have little control, it is at least no loss to try to bend things by words and gestures. If they do not work we are no worse off. Moreover, there is a gray area where we are not sure whether what we call "magic" does or does not work—in matters of illness, for example. Magic words may indeed have a healing effect, and a doctor's bedside manner is a distant relative of the witch doctor's healing formulae. But it is surely true that improvements in technology, for instance in agriculture, modify the use of such ritual techniques, and they begin to lose their prestige. Technology then itself becomes a new kind of magic.

The individual and personal counterpart to sacrifice is prayer, for this too is considered a way of opening up a path of communication with what lies Beyond. A good example of the logic of prayer is found in Islam. The Muslim who unrolls his prayer mat and bows down in the direction of Mecca is expressing quite a number of things. Have you noticed how Persian and other rugs from the Islamic world often have flowers and birds in their design? The reason is that a prayer rug is like a garden. Paradise is a garden too (the garden of Eden was Adam's paradise). Much of the Muslim world has sought to create a paradise on earth in gardens and courtyards. As the little poem has it, "You are closer to God in a garden/Than anywhere else on earth." So symbolically the Muslim makes a little oasis, a little heavenly place where he can pray. He unrolls his rug, marking off his sacred space from the profane space around him—be it street, a field, or an office floor. The pious Muslim gives himself a certain sacredness: He is slightly purified (at the mosque his preparations are more elaborate, and he washes himself to get himself in the proper state for communicating with Allah). He makes himself attractive to Allah, so as not to be repelled. When he bows down and touches his forehead on the ground he expresses in this bodily action his profound humility or "lowness" before God, thereby indicating Allah's vast, infinite superiority. Bowing in the direction of Mecca, he is directing himself in thought and by orientation toward the sacred stone there, which is the holiest place of contact between Allah and this earth. For him Mecca is the center of the cosmos and the place most charged with power and holiness. The city of Mecca is where Allah revealed himself primarily to the Prophet, so the contact between heaven and earth had its most dynamic expression there.

Also, in bowing toward Mecca the Muslim aligns himself with more than the place of revelation: He affirms his solidarity with all those others who face Mecca—with all his Islamic brothers, in other words. His prayer opens up a path to heaven—but by way of the community as well as the Prophet's message.

In essence, this account I have given so far of sacrifice and prayer follows the thinking of the French scholars Hubert and Mauss—who in 1898 published a famous essay on sacrifice—and to some degree that of Eliade. I have also incorporated some of my observations from my book, *The Concept of Worship* (1973).

In many cultures the formality with which sacrifice needs to be conducted (if it is to be properly acceptable) gives rise to a class of sacred specialists: priests. The person who offers a sacrifice may hire a priest to perform the task (a common feature of the Hindu tradition, which has given the priestly or Brahmin class the highest social and sacred status). But where the ritual is simpler and less formal, the individual can perform it effectively. An extreme form of informality is to be found among the Quakers, whose meetings have a spontaneous character: The group waits in silence for the Spirit to move one of its members to speak or lead a prayer.

In addition to sacrifices of the more literal kind in which an animal or other offering is made, the Catholic tradition has made use of the idea that the Mass is a kind of sacrifice. In commemorating the death and resurrection of Christ it relives the self-sacrifice that brought about a new relationship between God and the human race. Christ's death on the Cross is seen as a sacrifice (a kind of human sacrifice, we might say). The Mass re-presents this sacrifice. It makes it real here and now to the believer.

This points to another important aspect of ritual: A celebration of a rite is the re-creation of an event that myth describes, making it real now. It is as we have already seen, like time travel. The far-off past event becomes real to me *now*. The replay of the ancient drama is a contemporary event happening to me here and now. In Christianity, Jesus's death is seen not just as a historical event that happened a long time ago in Palestine, but as something present to the believer through ritual and inner experience here and now, in New York City or in Manchester, England, in the late part of the twentieth century.

Religions, as I have suggested, vary in the importance they attach to the formal and external aspects of ritual. There is a tug of war here. Consider a gift: I give something to a dear friend. It is a token of my friendship. But clearly the thought is important, the feeling behind the gift. On the one hand, the important thing is the inner feeling I have for my friend. On the other hand, the gift makes that feeling manifest. One reason for this is, in giving the other something I prize—suppose it is one of my favorite books—I give the other "a piece of myself," a little bit of me. Why? Because we think in a special way when it comes to possessions and people: We think according to the notions of "mystical participation," to use the phrase coined by the influential French anthropologist Lucien Lévy-Bruhl (1857–1939). (Strictly, it is the translation of his French phrase *participation mystique*.) My possessions are not quite separate things; they are part of a wider me. Try a little experiment. Leave a cheap ball point pen on a table, and watch your reactions if someone else picks it up. *My* pen, you think. How dare she take it! It is like an invasion of my space, or as if she had snipped off a bit of my hair. So the pen, trivial as it is, "mystically participates" in you, and you in the pen. Our truly valued possessions illustrate a much stronger bond, of course. A sacrifice, too, is "part of me," which I dedicate to a God or gods. It happens with groups as well, not just things. I am a Scotsman: In some way I mystically participate in Scottishness. If I hear other people insulting Scotsmen or Scotland I get upset. They are taking something of me and from me. Christ, in being human, participates in the human race, and the human race in him (thus goes the thought of much early Christian writing). In sacrificing himself he gives an offering on behalf of the human race which expiates the evil in which human beings are involved, through Adam and later generations.

So there is a way in which the concrete outer thing—the lamb sacrificed or the book I give to a friend—is a vital aspect of conveying feeling and opening communication. It is a symbol. It needs, however, to be accompanied (most of us tend to think) by sincere feelings. If I make no concrete gesture of contrition for some misdeed, then repentance is cheap. If all I have to do is make some external mechanical gesture, it may not be true contrition. Thus there is a tug of war between outer and inner. A gesture must be made, but that in itself is not enough; the gesture made must be sincere.

In Protestant Christianity and in Buddhism the emphasis, historically, was on inner feeling rather than outer formality. In the case of Reformation Protestantism salvation was thought to come from God and his grace alone. Attending Mass or performing pilgrimage could not in itself gain anyone spiritual advantages, and was, in fact, considered untrue to the gospel and to the sense of the numinous. The Protestant tradition has often stressed not outer ritual, but inner experience modeled on ritual; reliving the drama of baptism, for instance, by having the inner experience of being "born again." In the case of Buddhism, the rejection of sacrifices was in part due to the refusal to think in terms of mystical participation, which Buddhists thought leads to attachment to the world. If I get rid of "mystical participation" I am no longer attached to my book or my pen. Only by the purification of consciousness, and by the stilling of personal desire, do we attain liberation—not by any external acts.

This is not to say that there is no ritual in Buddhism. In later Buddhism there is a return to some of the Brahmin style of ritual thinking. At the time of the Buddha's death (ca. 483 B.C.E.) there was already the beginning of a cult around his ashes. They were distributed to *stūpas* or shrines, the predecessors of the modern temple and pagoda. The pious Buddhist pays reverence to the relic of a Buddha, or of some saint of times gone by. But on the whole, the Buddhist attitudes toward ritual are utilitarian. Ritual helps people to gain a better frame of mind. It does not bring about results in and of itself. In Sri Lanka, for instance, there is no question (at least in theory) of communicating with the Buddha as though he is a god who can be talked to in prayer, or acknowledged through sacrifices. At nirvana his individuality disappeared. There is no question of thinking of him as a continuing being. It is neither correct to say that he does exist nor that he does not. So ritual is not worship, but rather a skillful means of helping Buddhists on their upward and inward path.

Some of the logic of sacrifice carries over into modern secular ritual, particularly in regard to the nation and the state. Typically, a modern Western nation sets aside a day to commemorate those who have fallen in battle—Memorial Day in the United States, Armistice Day in the United Kingdom, and so on. Often, commemorating the dead by laying wreaths on some representative tomb or tombs, say, of the Unknown Soldier, is a means of paying homage to those who died for us. In doing so we renew our bonds with them. They in turn gain sacred stature from our reverence. We acknowledge the meaning of their sacrifice in battle. Dying for a nation enhances the substance of that nation. War itself, in causing people to die for the group, enhances the group. Similar thoughts apply to heroic, living achievements: Men on the moon enhance the prestige and substance of the nation that put them there. Much of the secular or "civil religion" (to use contemporary sociologist Robert Bellah's phrase) is a matter of performative acts that enhance the collective substance of society.

To sum up so far, sacrificial and other rituals are performative acts in which communication is established with the Beyond, or in the case of secular ritual, with the nation or group. In expressing ritual feelings, such as awe, something is conveyed—reverence for the divine Being, as in the Mass; or homage to the national spirit, as in a military parade. Rituals can be formal or informal. The emphasis in some religions is inner experience rather than outward acts or gestures.

Rites of Passage

Another important class of rituals is what have come to be known as rites of passage, following the work of the Belgian anthropologist Arnold van Gennep (1873–1957). These rites accompany vital transitions in life, as in puberty rites when young folk make the transition to adults; or as in baptism, when a person makes the transition from being outside to being inside the Christian community; or as in marriage, when two people move from one relationship to another. The rite is ceremony, or ritual, that marks a person's passage from one category to another.

Consider for a moment the difference between being a child and being an adult. Being a child means, among other things, that people *treat* you like a child. They may, for instance, "talk down" to you. Being an adult means that people usually treat you like an adult—it means that they have certain expectations of you. An adult is someone who can take a job, be married, and so on. The category "child" and the category "adult" are both charged with meanings that relate to the performative acts of, and for, children and adults.

They are "performative categories." That is, they are categories that define behavior in a given context. Virtually all our social categories, and many others, are performative. So if a person makes the transition from one category to another, it is important to mark the transition in some way. In many societies this is done very clearly and decisively through ritual. Thus, in many smaller societies, boys at puberty undergo various ordeals that do two things—they destroy their old identity as children and prepare them for their new responsibilities as adults. Such a ritual typically involves three stages: first, separation from the old; second, a limbo stage, called "liminal" (after the Latin word *limen*, a threshold, for the person is, as it were, crossing the threshold); and third, the stage of being incorporated into the new identity.

We can see something of this in the rituals associated with marriage. The night before the wedding, the bridegroom has a party with his men friends. Such a stag party is a farewell to the unmarried, bachelor state, a final "night out with the boys." The bride, when she comes to the church, is "given away" by her father, signaling that she is leaving the pure daughterly state and becoming something else. In the ceremony itself the performative utterance "I promise" seals the bond. The feast after the ceremony is itself a kind of limbo. It is secular, and yet the bride stays in her ceremonial dress. Then the pair leave for the honeymoon. This is a kind of sacred interlude, the truly liminal phase, when the pair are out of sight in some unusual place that is neither their old home nor their new dwelling. The end of this liminal phase occurs when the bridegroom, now the husband, carries his wife over the threshold and they set up home together. Now, because they are husband and wife, they are treated differently by the rest of the community. The new spouses are now the married couple. In modern society, with people living together before marriage, or without being married, the categories get blurred, and this very blurring sometimes creates performative awkwardness.

It is also interesting how a new category can be formed out of what before might have been thought of as betwixt-and-between. Thus, in traditional society hostility to homosexuals can occur because people wish to work with two clearly defined categories, male and female. The adult who has some male properties and also some female ones becomes a threat to the two-category system. So he is rejected, or she is, by performative acts designed to exclude or humiliate her or him. However, such ritual rejections can be met by a counterattack. This is what has occurred in recent times by Gay Liberation tactics, which essentially are ritual tactics—first the use of positive performative words such as "gay" rather than "queer"; second by demonstrations expressing gay solidarity and defying older conventions. The result is to begin to establish along with male and female heterosexuality a third, intermediate category, namely "gay."

The extension of childhood and of education has also led to some blurring of the child versus adult distinction, and slowly we have developed a third and intermediate category, the "teenager." But it remains an awkward age, for the social roles of the teenager are often conflicting. Which is he or she—child or adult? How is he or she to be treated? Many older societies seem to have ignored this category altogether. In India, for instance, child marriage was the norm; if marriage was arranged before puberty, the intermediate stage, with all of its conflicting social roles, was abolished.

In religious rites of passage the symbolism is often complex. Thus, the rite of baptism in the Christian tradition signals, in essence, the transition from solidarity with the old Adam to solidarity with the new Adam, Christ. In baptism by immersion, a person goes down into the water, the symbol of chaos and death—although it is also the symbol of purification because by water we become clean. The person thus dies with Christ, crosses a threshold, and rises again to life with Christ through his resurrection, thus becoming part of the new community that is linked in substance with the Lord. Christ is seen as the vine and the individual Christians are the branches, so that the Church is, in a sense, part of Christ. Typical of such ideas of "mystical participation" is the thought that the Church both is and is not Christ, as my pen (in the earlier example) is and is not part of me. At any rate baptism brings on new life within the community, and death to the old self. It also gives the person access to the sacramental life of the Church.

The betwixt-and-between, or liminal state, is regarded as full of power, but it may be holy power that is manifested there, or something unpleasantly dangerous. So it is with people who fall between categories: Jesus, for instance, who is both God and human being, whose mysterious words and actions were regarded by some as full of holiness and by others as dangerous.

As we have seen in the case of Buddhism, rituals can be used to bring about certain states of mind. They are important more for their results than for their inner meaning, in such a case. For instance, if I lay flowers before a statue of the Buddha, I feel serene and gain merit, and my action is important for its effect on me. There is a difference here between religious practices related to the experience of the numinous, and those with a more mystical, inner direction. For the religion of the numinous, worship is a response (to the overwhelming Other) that is in itself appropriate. It is the proper response to the sacred and powerful, much as we might think that an exclamation of admiration is the proper response to a beautiful sunset. The admiration does not bring the sunset about. It reflects it, tries to give it its due, so to speak. But often in Buddhism and elsewhere, things are the other way around: The doctrines and the practices are the proper ones because they help to bring about the purified and luminous consciousness that induces peace and insight. They are proper teachings and methods of mind control and physical technique, such as breathing in a certain way, because they engineer the experience of the Void.

In Islamic and Christian mysticism matters are more complex, for the acts of prayer and the ascetic practices that stem from extreme piety and devotion to God turn, little by little, into techniques of contemplation. When this happens, worship and mysticism blend, and the numinous response mingles with the mystical method.

At a less dramatic level, ritual such as solemn worship helps to engender as well as to express feelings of the awesome majesty of God. Hymns help to heighten people's sense of the unseen. Icons and other kinds of art become pointers to the Beyond. Art itself is brought into the service of religious practice. This indeed may go a long way back in human history. There are, on either side of the Pyrenees and elsewhere in Europe, those famous caves where old paintings of magnificent animals and strange human figures could be seen by the flickering light of ancient hunters' torches. What do these mysterious drawings, with animals and other outlined figures sometimes imposed one on top of the other, really mean? We may never find out for sure, but the evidence suggests that the very act of making these pictures was itself sacred. Art was seen as a way of creating a response to the strange forces surrounding the human race.

Increasingly, modern religion has come to give weight to inner experience, whether it is the sense of being born again, or the sense of gaining illumination and vision. The popularity of forms of Zen Buddhism and other Eastern mysticism in the 1960s and 1970s was a reflection of the fact that Western people more and more felt a need for authenticity, to cut through the formal ritual of much organized religion, and to find the meaning of faith vividly in personal experience. This personal side to religion is likely to lead more and more to the feeling that rituals really have their ultimate meaning in experience. They gain their validity from the feelings they evoke and the visions they help create.

The "sanctity" of the ritual dimension of existence seems to apply in even the most secular contexts. For, as we have seen, rituals help to create and preserve categories. One category of the most fundamental importance in the world is the category of *person*. But what, in the last resort, is a person? A person is a living being of a certain kind, but more than that he or she is a living being who is to be treated in a certain way, with dignity and as a being whose feelings matter. There are, as we saw earlier, performative acts that are proper responses to her as a person: He or she is not to be humiliated through acts of discourtesy and disdain, but rather to be given the sense that others prize him or her. Ultimately that is how we all would wish to be treated. As it is, much in modern life denies such treatment—huge economic forces can bear impersonally upon us; many governments practice torture, imprisonment, and other kinds of humiliation in a reckless and widespread way; and some political philosophies deal in the abstractions of revolution as if human beings can be discarded when necessary. All such assaults on persons are, among other things, ritual assaults, or failures to give due ritual recognition to the individual. They are failures in courtesy, gentleness, and the assigning of respect and dignity to human beings. In short, the very idea of a person is itself a performative concept. We gain our substance from the courtesies and loving gestures we extend to one another.

Thus it is that the ritual and ethical dimensions of life go together. Kant's notion that we should treat others never merely as means, but always as ends in themselves, is a call for us to show others, through personal acts, that they have dignity and are worthy of our personal concern. In Christian and Jewish terms we can say that every person is made in the image of God, and that as we worship the Creator we venerate the reflection of the divine in one another. And what does it mean to venerate? It is implicitly to show, in gesture, our sense of the sacred character of that which we venerate. Veneration belongs to the ritual dimension of religion.

The ritual and ethical dimensions cannot exist except in the social context, as we have suggested. So let us now move on to sketch that social dimension of religion and existence.

Chapter

8

The Social Dimension

In a small-scale society—the sort of ethnic group anthropologists have most liked to study—there is typically a single overarching worldview. Individuals may have variations in belief, and some may have their skeptical impulses, but on the whole such a society has a single system of religious beliefs. Most larger societies are different, for various reasons. For one thing, as we have seen, nation-states increasingly display great internal pluralism—that is, they include a variety of minorities, often from afar. Such a society has within it a mosaic of worldviews.

Second, the increase in division between Church—or mosque, or temple—and State (true in the modern West and some Eastern and other countries) means that citizens can, both inwardly and outwardly, affirm different beliefs, including the rejection of all formal systems of belief.

Third, many modern industrial societies have undergone much secularization, in the sense that many people are alienated, or at least distanced, from formal religion or ideology. In many societies, then, a division exists between those who are "committed" to a religious or other belief-system, and those who are not. Not surprisingly, in modern times Western religion has stressed faith and commitment. For a person must have faith and commitment if he or she is to be distinctly religious. In many a traditional society, including the small-scale ones of the past (for things are changing there too), a person was brought up with a set of values, including religious ones. For traditional Italy it was quite "natural" to be Catholic. Catholicism was assumed, as it was assumed that a Romanian would be Orthodox or an Iraqi Muslim. But, in modern societies this is not always the case.

Modern Social Theories

Anthropologists have been good at seeing the way the different parts of society fit together, and how the whole works. Religion often has been explained as having a vital social function. One theory, called *functionalism*, purports that society and its many diverse components, among them religion, can be understood according to the functions, or needs, they fulfill, and thereby help to maintain social equilibrium. Functionalism's most important founding father was the French Jewish social theorist Émile Durkheim (1858–1917). He had trained to become a rabbi. Seeing belief in supernatural beings as something with no clear basis in reason, he sought to explain religion as a reflection of social values. He was thus a prime exponent of projectionism which, as we have seen, has played so strong a part in the development of psychological and sociological approaches to religion in modern times. In a way, Durkheim was drawing a picture of society that was a secularized version of the Jewish community. Now the giver of the law is not Yahweh but society itself, which secretly disguises the origin of its values. They might appear to come from on high but actually, argued Durkheim, they come from within.

Modern structuralism, too, has come out of the anthropological tradition. Structuralism attempts to see the structures that underlie myths and other aspects of a given culture, as well as the ways in which they are integrated together. Claude Lévi-Strauss (b. 1908) in a number of highly potent writings described how we can see various polarities in myth and in society as reflecting a deep-seated mode of thinking. Structuralism is a way of trying to piece together the logic of stories that otherwise seem mysterious and chaotic, by bringing various symmetries and problems to the surface. This method, although useful in interpreting myths, is not a way of explaining myth and religion as a reflection of their social function.

Rather, it is a way of showing how the various parts of a culture hang together. It is easier to work out structural patterns in a single integrated culture, and so structuralism is a method peculiarly relevant to the anthropologist.

But although the work of anthropologists has deeply affected the study of religion, the great religions have had a different shape from that of religions in small-scale societies. While in small-scale societies religion is part of the fabric of society, the great religions often started within societies as novel forces, challenging the assumptions of the rest of society. When religions start—early Christianity, Buddhism, and Islam for instance—they have not been concerned so much with maintaining equilibrium as with providing—in a revolutionary way—a new way of looking at the world and at society. For another thing such religions typically migrate from one society to another: They have a missionary outreach. Again, they have tended to create a deeper sense of their own distinct history than is usual in the functional religions of smaller ethnic groups. In a word, they have a more plural and more dynamic context. Thus sociologists have become more and more interested in the way religions and worldviews create, or inhibit, change. This was true already in the writings of Marx, for although religion might often have a conservative role, ideas themselves were one ingredient in those changes by which a new phase of the historical process unfolds.

This interest in the creative role of religion is evident in the ample writings of Max Weber (1864–1920). As we saw earlier, he questioned why the rise of capitalism happened in the West, and how much the Reformation had influenced it. He saw Luther's work as helping to clear away the old order. On the one hand, Luther's stress on faith directly suggested that salvation is an individual matter. The individual is thus a key element in a society. The rise of individualism meant many things, among them modernization, and flexibility in the use of human resources. We can see how Luther's teaching thus favored the rise of the urban middle class that was so vital a factor in the creation of capital.

Luther's rebellion against the Papacy, the support he received from German princes, together with his own contributions to the modern German language, particularly through his translation of the Bible—all helped the development of national consciousness. Nationalism was to play a strong role in modernization. In some of the new nationalisms of northern Europe—in Holland and England, for example—mercantile activity and Protestant religion interacted powerfully. Beyond Lutheranism, the new Calvinism provided an even more complete worldview that could favor capitalism. No longer was the ascetic life something lived in monasteries. The Christian lived vigorously in the world and at the same time was not "of it." The sobriety of the citizen of the new community helped the accumulation of savings and capital. The Protestant community was not lavish with display and ceremony and spending great wealth on cathedrals and festivals. But having individual wealth might be a sign of God's favor.

Conversely, Weber was intent on showing that the forces that brought about capitalism in the West were not present in India or China, but that there were other, countervailing forces. Confucianism, though rational and "this-worldly," was at the same time deeply wedded to a classical order in which the gentleman scholar, well-versed in ancient writings, was the key figure. Hinduism's caste system gave restrictive roles to the various strata of society, keeping artisans to traditional tasks and merchants to a particular status.

More recently, the economic miracle of Japan has spurred questions of how far its Buddhist, Confucian, and Shinto heritages have helped to account for this success. Was Buddhism's special development in Japan toward a this-worldly Zen a factor? Does the idea that Buddhism uses "skill in means" to achieve its message give Japanese society a pragmatic slant? Does Confucianism, once released from the inhibitions imposed by the old educational system, encourage a new sense of hard work and order? There is a growing interest among economists in those deep cultural factors that may lie behind economic development.

This discussion of the relationship between economics, society, and religion shows us that the essential question regarding the social dimension of religion is this: To what extent is religion a reflection of what goes on in the structures of society, and to what extent does it bring these structures about? Or to put it more directly: What effects does religion have? Or is it itself just an effect?

Naturally, these questions are put too simply. We are always concerned not with religion as such, but with a particular religion, a particular society or group of societies. And we may not be dealing even with a particular religion but, more accurately, with a particular movement, sect, or denomination. It may even be that we are not so much dealing with an institutionalized form of religion, but rather with a kind of religious experience or a particular symbol or an idea. There is no doubt, for instance, that the writer Alan Watts (1915–1973), who was a guru of Eastern spirituality (which he blended with his own values and Anglo-American background), had

an influence on the counterculture and the turbulent events of the
late 1960s and early 1970s in America. He established no denomination, no church, but rather articulated and promoted some ideas,
an atmosphere, a slant on life, a worldview. None of it constituted
an institution, yet all of it had an effect. And at the same time, Alan
Watts' own experience was conditioned by his times—the times he
himself helped create.

Social Theories of Religion

The social exploration of religion often has to be very particular and
limited. Yet by examining specific events, ideas, and expressions we
may venture on some more general reflections and theories.

American sociologist Peter Berger (b. 1929) in his book *The
Sacred Canopy* and elsewhere has written of the "methodological
atheism" of the sociologist. It is better to use the expression
"methodological agnosticism." The point Berger wished to make is
that the sociologist does not bring God into his account of how
things happen. He does not assume the existence of God in order to
explain events. It is one thing not to assume that God does exist; it
is another thing to assume that he does not. If we assume, more
generally, that there is no Ultimate, no Beyond, then we assume
that religion is false. Religion, then, is a finger that points, but at
nothing. There is no moon for it to point to. It does not seem especially scientific to begin with the assumption that religion is false,
nor need we begin with the assumption that it is true. What we are
concerned with is not the truth of religion, but its power. If we are
adhering to a scientific stance or methodology, we should be neutral
regarding the truth or falsity of religion; we should be neutral as to
whether the finger points at the moon beyond or at nothing. This is
why it is better to speak of "methodological agnosticism": The
agnostic has not decided whether God exists; the theist and the
atheist have.

The chief object of the social-scientific study of religion is to
see how the social dimension relates in influence and power to the
other dimensions. There is, however, an ambiguity in the idea of the
social dimension.

Religion can be so deeply integrated into social life, as in many
small-scale societies, that it is impossible to isolate and study as a
distinct phenomenon. It is an aspect of the life of the group. But it
is sometimes the case that religion exists as a separate institution,
part of and yet independent from the rest of society. Thus in

Western countries there are separate religious organizations, old and new—here we mean everything from the Catholic Church, to many small denominations and sects, to new religious movements, to religions coming from foreign cultures. When I talk about the social dimension of religion I may be referring to religion in a broad social context; or I may be referring to the actual institutions themselves.

Thus, American religion—say American Catholicism—is not merely institutionalized in a certain way: There is a broader significance that religion has in American society. American Catholicism contributes to American social processes and at the same time is affected by them. For instance, it affects attitudes on issues of abortion, and it has contributed many notable figures to American political and cultural life. Conversely, American democratic ideals and American culture have influenced American Catholicism—consider how Catholic education, armed with American football and Notre Dame, reflects a blend between American and Catholic values. If we are thinking of societies that are not integral, like small-scale societies of the past, then the social dimension is, more narrowly considered, the way in which a religion is institutionalized. More widely considered, the social dimension is the social role in the wider society that the religion plays. A major part of the sociology of religion is devoted to the question, How far does the institutional dimension of a religion affect the wider society and how far does the wider society affect it?

We have been looking at worldviews in general, not just confining our attention to traditional religions or religion in the traditional sense. A similar approach to that taken above can be taken in looking at institutionalized worldviews of a secular kind. Thus, we may consider how successful the Chinese Communist Party has been in reshaping the values of Chinese society, and how far the cult of Chairman Mao was able to maintain some of the initial élan and drive of the revolution. In short, are some of the same things happening in China as are happening in the evolution of a church or religious movement? We have the founding charismatic hero (St. Francis or Mao); the charisma becomes something not personal but is "routinized" through the ongoing institution; and there arises a division of followers into those who pragmatically adhere to the routines, and others, more radical, who try to recapture the spirit of the "early days."

This idea of charisma (a word derived from the New Testament and referring there to what is given through God's grace) was first elaborated in a systematic way by Max Weber in his account of the evolution of religious institutions. For religions, with all their appeal to the past, actually tend to run in cycles, in which first a key role is played by the prophet or mystic as blazer of a new trail. In the ensuing period the preservation of this insight, and the evolving pattern of religion, can lead to a traditionalism that does not quite match the breathless novelty of the original message. So the tradition prepares for polarity and a possible struggle: In preserving the founder's message it preserves a memory of revolution, but in being faithful and conservative it creates a layer of traditionalism. The time bomb ticks away until a new prophet or mystic arises who may latch on to the quiet forces of revolution.

For a new revolution to be effective one needs the right conditions. It is said, "Cometh the hour, cometh the man." It is equally so the other way around: "Cometh the man, cometh the hour." Thus we can point to forerunners of the Protestant Reformation, but various sorts of kindling were required in order for Luther's spark to create the blaze. So far as we can figure out from the ancient records, the period of the Buddha was "right" for him. There were cities expanding along the banks of the Ganges and nearby that contained a growing new mercantile class to whom the Buddhist teaching appealed. For one thing, Buddhism made much of giving, but little of sacrificial ritual. The "new men" of the emerging culture along the Ganges could free themselves from the entangling taboos of the Brahmins and, in acquiring merit by supporting the Buddhist Order, assure themselves of a better life. When we see the rise of a new religion we are wise to look to the social conditions that favored it. In modern times we can likewise ask: What are the appealing factors in the cults or new religious movements? How do they match certain social needs?

We can see various ways in which religion is relatively dependent and relatively dynamic. Is it importing its values from society, or is it, on balance, exporting them?

In more detail, of course, one can see how religion works in a particular region or for particular social groups. After all, if a religious movement attracts people it may be because it is responsive to their needs and slant on life. It is interesting to investigate the social and psychological background of those who join a particular group, such as the Unification Church or Zen Centers or Orthodox Judaism.

Sometimes such affinity is a matter of personality type. But it can also and more frequently be seen in social terms. Thus studies at various times have shown that, in American society, there is more interest in religious questions among women than among men. This fact was brought out clearly by Gerhard Lenski (b. 1924) in a study conducted in 1953. There may be two explanations, given the position of women at that time. First, women have a greater part to play in bringing up children, and the question of how to prepare the young for life tends to raise questions about religious tradition and the ultimate. Second, women—having less power—are from one perspective a minority group, and religion is often a means of expressing the predicament of those who feel themselves "underdogs." A study of whether women's liberation has made substantial differences to the position of women would tell us if these hypotheses about the function of religion are valid.

Religion, Society, and the Secular State

The connection of religion and oppression is strong in Marx. This has led to some embarrassing questions about the survival of religion in supposed Marxist societies. In theory, since religion represents the sign of the oppressed creature and the opium of the people, the need for it should wither away in a socialist context. But in fact some paradoxes exist in the actual development of religion under socialist regimes.

If we look to Poland and Romania, the one Catholic and the other Eastern Orthodox, there can be little doubt that the great piety and solidarity of the people of these countries in the practice of their faith owes much to nationalism. But the survival of religion in these countries also perhaps reflects the fact that there are aspects of life which the state belief-system cannot easily cope with. Each individual, for example, has to come to terms with death, whatever the social system. The rituals could seem rich and illuminating in comparison with the drab life of the old socialist system and the hardships brought in with the attempt to found a new market economy.

There is an ambiguity in the notion of "secular" society. Often when we think about the secularization of life, we think of ways in which traditional religious values and practices no longer have the same power. The older peasant culture of Europe, for instance, was soaked in the rhythms of religious life, but with the Industrial Revolution, and before that the Reformation, much of that older religious life began to wane. For one thing, the rhythms of the city were different from those of the countryside. For another, the older, extended family ties, which themselves had religious roots and expression, began to weaken with the new mobility of the industrial society. Then again, the new forms of social and economic organization promised a richer life here and now. By the early twentieth century, in America and elsewhere, the dream of "a chicken in every pot and a car in every garage" came to be a way of making the pursuit of happiness—the creed of the new society—more concrete. Thus, from one angle secularization means a drift from traditional religious customs and ideas: instead of feast days, football games; instead of pilgrimages, tourism; instead of cathedrals, movie theaters; instead of penances, diets; instead of hymns, the Beatles; instead of God, love; instead of crusades, war; instead of Christendom, the nation; instead of the Bible, the newspaper; instead of prayer, television; instead of salvation, happiness; instead of peace of mind, fun; instead of confession, psychoanalysis; instead of sin, problems; instead of the Second Coming, progress.

But there is another meaning of the term "secular" that is different, though connected. A secular state is one with no official religion. There was a time when, to be a citizen in good standing in Sweden, you had to be a Lutheran, in Spain a Catholic, in Egypt a Muslim. The assumption was that a regime required religious sanction and that sanction should be recognized by all those loyal to the regime. So Catholics were often expelled from England, Jews from Spain, and so on. But toleration, pioneered in England from 1688 onward, in America from its beginnings, and in France after the revolution, came to be the hallmark of the modern liberal state. Such a state might retain some acknowledgment of the primacy of some religious denomination, but in practice allows for a variety of beliefs, including atheism. Thus, in an American state university, for example, though there may be Religious Studies as a wide and impartial department exploring religion and religions, there cannot be denominational teaching. You cannot preach Judaism or Christianity as if this were the religion of the state. If you want to be confessional in education, you have to "go private." This system, with the state being neutral and "above" religions, is what we refer to as the "secular state."

In this second sense you may have a secular state with a very nonsecular population, as in the Republic of India, which is more or less neutral in matters of religion, unlike Pakistan, which is a religiously defined nation with an Islamic constitution. India is overwhelmingly religious, mainly Hindu, but with a vast Muslim minority and groups such as Sikhs, Parsees, and Christians as well.

Whereas the secular state occurs chiefly in the West, with variations in Africa and elsewhere, the most important type of rule matching the older religious states is the modern Marxist regime. There the citizen is expected to conform to the official worldview. If a person is a pious Christian or Buddhist he may be thwarted in his career. A friend of mine was imprisoned in a European Communist state for being an active Buddhist. The situation is like that of England, Spain, or Egypt, once upon a time. In fact, it may be a more intense version of the old system because authoritative control—spying on citizens, for example—is now more efficient than it was.

Such a system may be called "monistic" (i.e., unitary in belief) in contrast to the pluralism of the secular state. So one meaning of "secular" is roughly "nontraditionally religious." The other meaning is "nonmonistic." In a "monistic" state (which is not secular in the sense in which the Western democracy is) the ideals may be secular in the sense of being modern, nontraditional, and antireligious. The ideal Soviet man was pictured with a tool or a gun ready to work or do battle for the revolution, armed with new technology, turning his back heroically upon the oppressive and pious past, no longer in need of the "opium" of the people, with no interest in the Beyond, only in the shining future in which a new world is being fashioned. Similar things can be said concerning the new ideals of China, both under and after Mao.

But the two senses of secularization are connected, for the effect of toleration and other forces in the modern secular state tends to make traditional religion an *option*. There are many choices within it, for there are many varieties of religion to choose from. Faith becomes increasingly a private affair, and this tends to erode traditionalism. Older religions become denominations within a wider whole. Making religion a private matter can also lead to religion's becoming just a minor element in a total fabric of living. Just as a person belongs to the golf club, so he may join a church.

A major task of the sociology of religion is to plot the kinds of changes affecting religion in the modern world. Among these secularization, as in the growth of nontraditional attitudes, is obviously important in the Western world. Moreover, it is not a matter just of seeing how far traditional attitudes persist. They change under the impact of new forces. This is evident in the way new religious movements have arisen in Africa and other southern regions of the world. It is evident too in the way in which older religions, such as Hinduism, have adapted to the challenge of the West and to the impact of modern science and technology. Hinduism has fashioned for itself a new philosophy based on old sources in which religion and science are seen as differing responses to the same cosmos, which to the eye of the mystic and the devotee is divine—and to the eye of the scientist is a material order to be understood and controlled.

Those who hold that religion can be explained by its social function like to think of the new religious movements of the small-scale societies as responses to dislocations: They spring in a sense from the fact that a society is threatened from outside, fails to function properly, and needs some new solution. This new solution is often a fantasy solution (according to this view), but it is in a sense an expression and projection of the sense of struggle the society is facing. Thus many movements combine magic and the idea of a millennium, a new social order of prosperity and peace. In New Guinea and other parts of Melanesia in the South Pacific in this century there have been a number of so-called cargo cults, in which the hope of magical access to the White Man's goods (often thought to have been stolen from the ancestors of the natives) arises, leading to a new social order in which the natives live at ease and in harmony. We might see such cults as using elements from the natives' understanding of life in order to deal with the dislocations caused by the incoming white man.

The hope of a new social order coming through divine action is not something new. It was part of the hope of the early Christians and of various sections within the contemporary Jewish community. It is a way in which people draw substance and power from the future. The Melanesian who constructs a "magical" airfield in the hope that planes will land there with goods that until now only the whites have had access to may seem naive; but we should not forget that the ideal of a New Jerusalem built in our own country is one of the potent dreams which has drawn Western civilization forward. The question, though, is how such dreams can be used creatively. The cargo cults are doomed to disappointment when interpreted just in terms of commodities. But the dream of a new community was used creatively by the Mormons—and without that dream there would have been no Utah as we know it today.

Because the peoples of the world are in close interaction, with new forces continuously being brought to bear on every society (with smaller societies particularly feeling the strain), there is a wide spectrum of new religious movements. This suggests new ways in which the social sciences may be illuminating. For we may learn lessons from the way some of these movements develop and apply this knowledge to the historical understanding of older faiths in their early days. We may have a better understanding, for instance, of Christianity when it was a "new religious movement."

Indeed, we can apply various categories to such movements. It is useful at this point to go back to a distinction between the Church and the sect made by Ernst Troeltsch (1865–1923), a Christian theologian who took sociology seriously. The distinction between these two types of religious organization, together with the related notions of the denomination and the cult, have been prominent in sociological study. The sociology of religion, however, remains overcommitted to Western language, reflecting the special experience of the Christian tradition, and the terminology does not fit at all well in Eastern and other non-Christian contexts. However, Troeltsch's distinctions represent a beginning of classification. One point has to be made before we proceed: Weber, Troeltsch, and others used what can be called "ideal types" to classify and illuminate data. The ideal type is a model that may not be a full portrait—indeed, it cannot be a full portrait—of the complexities of actual institutions. But the model serves as a useful simplification to help us understand the data more broadly than would otherwise be possible. "Church" and "sect" are ideal types in this sense.

The Church as an institution both dominates and is dominated by the social structure in which it finds itself. It dominates because it seeks to permeate the whole of a society and to use its influence to make society more Christian (or more Buddhist, for example, if we are thinking of the Sangha in Sri Lanka or Thailand). It is dominated by society in the sense that it necessarily takes on some of society's characteristics. Thus, the early Christians did not have a church in this sense: Their movement was akin to today's sects. But Christianity came to be the religion of the Roman Empire, and in so doing the Roman world became Catholic and Catholicism itself became Roman. By contrast, the sect is more in the nature of a counterculture. It tends to reject a church's compromise with the world. It stresses ideal behavior and a closed circle, to which admittance is by conversion (while, by contrast, one tends to be "born into" a church).

Sometimes sects accept society and affirm its goals, but see their own prescriptions as better ways to achieve them. Christian Science and Transcendental Meditation, for example, believe that they have certain special ways of enhancing health and life in society. Sometimes they substitute for worldliness a superior ethic in which a community, more or less uncontaminated by the world, seeks salvation—this is a common feature of communal groups. The commune is often seen as the ideal society within society. The sect, then, is very much an in-group. A good instance are the Jehovah's Witnesses, with their predictions of the end of history and the taking up of those who are saved (the rest of the world perishing without a trace). There are also sects that are, in principle or in practice, at odds with society, and that seek to change it radically, possibly by rebellion and upheaval. A secular variety of this type was found among the Italian Red Brigades and other leftist terrorist groups in Europe—revolutionary sects who suppose that through chaos they will bring about the collapse of the existing order and the coming into being of a new, more just society. Sects of this type often aggressively seek conversion, in their hope to radically change society.

Between the sect and the Church there lies the denomination. This is, so to speak, an organizationally separate branch of the Church. Unlike the sect, the denomination has a certain degree of integration into the wider society. What in one country may be a church can, in a more plural setting, become a denomination. In America, for example, Catholicism is a denomination somewhat on par with other Christian denominations, although other parts of the Roman Catholic Church (in Spain and Italy, for example) are in the relevant sense *churches*.

More recently it has been fashionable in Western contexts to add the category "cult"—a sect in the making, such as the Moonies, the Hare Krishna, and the Scientologists. Most have charismatic leaders. There does not seem to be any great reason to treat them differently from sects (they may in time become "normalized" within society and become denominations). Some of these movements need to be understood in a wider context than a single society or nation. They are transnational. They are attempts to weave together elements from differing social and cultural backgrounds. The Moonies (followers of the Reverend Sun Myung Moon) incorporate ideas from the Confucian tradition as well as evangelical Christianity into a new mixture with its own particular dynamic. The Hare Krishna movement takes on more than Indian qualities in the context of New York and San Francisco.

We live at a time when the opportunities are unique for seeing the way religions and worldviews change through their interaction and migration. Already the study is beginning of how religions react when they have an extensive diaspora, that is, where adherents live scattered in foreign places and cities; for example, Hinduism in Fiji and Guyana, Buddhism among Vietnamese in Los Angeles, Chinese worldviews in Singapore and San Francisco, Islam in Britain and Germany, Zulu religion in the cities of South Africa, and so on. Moreover, we have unfolding before us many movements in which elements from different traditions are put together as ways of reacting, sometimes creatively, to the problems raised by the collision of differing cultures and life styles.

Clearly, religion itself is deeply affected by social change, and new movements arise and grow from the challenges of change and interaction. But these new movements have their own dynamic, in tapping reserves of myth and symbolism and creating new combinations of values. Often the charismatic leader is a person who somehow experiences in his own life some of the tensions that he seeks to express and to cope with, on a larger scale, as a religious leader; in this way he often unknowingly prepares the way for a new social pattern.

We have here sketched briefly some of the ways in which the social sciences can approach the religious factor in human life. The social approach to religion can help us to reflect upon the future of religion and some of the larger issues raised by its study.

For the fact is that religion is itself affected by the new perspectives we are continually gaining by studying it. We are in this as in other areas of human life coming to a new kind of self-consciousness. To some thoughts about the future of religious and other worldviews I now turn.

Chapter

9

Reflections on the Future of Religion and Ideology

Many educated people in the West, impressed by the increasing secularization of society and by their own view that religious tradition no longer has much intellectual power, have tended to think that the study of religion is rather old-fashioned. It might be able to tell us some fascinating things about the human past, but it does not promise to unlock many secrets of the future. Even now throughout the world of English-speaking philosophy there is a wide dismissal of religion as irrational, and many of those affected by the tradition of Marx and Freud think that traditional religion is bound to fade. Yet there are, as we have seen, forces—both rational and emotional—that suggest otherwise.

For one thing, some of the secular gods have shown clay feet. Consider the dreadful fate of Cambodia after the success of the Khmer Rouge takeover in 1975. Here was a social revolution guided by a new secular ideology based on principles worked out by the French-educated leader Khieu Samphan. It was not orthodox Marxism. Rather it was an antitraditional attempt to produce a rural-based Communist society totally cut off from the outside world—particularly from the capitalist system that was seen as part of that colonial past, and that had led to the bleeding of Cambodia and its corruption by French and other cultural influences. The 1970s revolution produced untold misery. Its end came with an invasion by Moscow-allied Communists from Vietnam who practiced a secular ideology of such harshness that hundreds of thousands of people from Vietnam took to perilous boats across the South China Sea in order to escape. The initial success of the Khmer Rouge had partly to do with American bombing and other incursions, which prevented Cambodia's survival as a neutral nation. Such intervention, under the orders of then-President Nixon and Secretary of State Kissinger, could in a sense have been well-meaning. It was all done in defense of the Western democratic ideals of freedom, and it was done with the careless and cruel confidence of those who think that military-technological power can solve most problems. Cambodia is a tragic example of the effects of secular ideologies launched without regard for the people who must then live with them. The Khmer Rouge had a creed that was mad and unrealistic; the Vietnamese creed was cruel; the Buddhists' was too passive; and the Americans' too technocratic.

The environmentalist movement, from the late 1960s onward, has also been a sign of the crumbling of older kinds of materialism and of the easy dismissal of religion. The view that nature is just material, waiting to be shaped and exploited on behalf of the human race, has given way to a new vision of the webs that bind together the different forms of life in their environment and that thus bind together both organic and inorganic nature. This perception of the flow back and forth between us and nature owes something to Eastern religious influence. Edward Schumacher's pioneering book *Small Is Beautiful* was greatly influenced by Buddhism; other authors have been influenced by Taoism and Native American and other traditions. Thus it is incorrect to assume that it is more "rational" to adopt a materialist worldview that dismisses traditional religious values.

The fact is that religion survives and has frequent revivals. Although there have been severe attempts to suppress it in modern times in the old Soviet Union and in China, religion has reemerged with a fair amount of vigor. It looks as if secular ideologies, including Western scientific humanism, do not cater to the full emotional and ritual needs of human beings. Western liberal democracy can create the "lonely crowd" and the sense of a loss of identity. Secular creeds on the whole ignore the necessity of facing death and suffering. They also ignore spiritual experience and its meaning for humanity.

At the same time, nationalism remains a force of great emotional power. For many people "freedom" and "liberation" refer not to personal freedom or individual liberation, but rather to the liberation of the national group. Every self-respecting oppressed ethnic group has a "national liberation front." Nor should we underestimate, especially in the Southern Hemisphere, the continued appeal of Marxism as a way of solving social and economic problems in emerging countries—especially those that link their oppression to the colonial past and to the Western countries, and therefore to capitalism. We shall continue to live in a world where traditional religion and the secular ideologies will be in powerful interplay.

Does our study of religion and worldviews suggest how human beliefs will develop? And in what sort of world?

It seems clear from past and present developments that the unfolding of future religion will occur within a new wider community—the totality of the globe, what I have called the "global city." Religion and the secular ideologies find themselves more and more in a state of self-consciousness. They look at themselves in a mirror. The very attempt to explore religions and to analyze worldviews produces images that in turn affect those religions and worldviews. The maturing disciplines of the social and human sciences have done much, in the last century and in this one, to influence such attitudes. We know more about our own history than any previous generation. We know more about populations, shifts in economic behavior, changes in marriage customs—more, in short, about the varieties of society in the world than was ever possible in the past. We know more about the religions of the world, and we know more about revolutions, governments, bureaucracies, voting preferences, political attitudes, than ever before. We know more about patterns of human belief and action than was possible in pre-modern times. We see ourselves—sometimes clearly, sometimes not so clearly—in the new intellectual mirrors we have made.

There are two sides to this tremendous explosion of knowledge— one connected with the global city, the other to the questions of truth and analysis. On the one side, the very knowledge we have becomes a mode of introducing cultures to one another, and so of opening these cultures to influences that bring changes. I was involved in being general adviser to the BBC television series *The Long Search*. This series reached millions of people in and beyond the English-speaking world. It affected, among others, an aunt of mine, the widow of a Scottish Presbyterian minister, and a fine person. She said she had not known how much good there was in Buddhism and other religions of the East. Already her attitude toward Christianity was being slightly modified. Such communication systems as television and books, and the migrations of individuals and groups, have the effect of opening up paths between faiths that affect those faiths. They will never again simply be able to ignore one another naturally, and cutting a faith off from the rest of the world will result in a new kind of global sectarianism. (The Ayatollah's Iran is in danger thus of becoming, as it were, a global sect.)

On the other side, there are questions about the rationality of religion and about the validity of religious experiences and symbols. For, in a world in which more and more people are experiencing the effects of science and are being introduced to a scientific education, issues of religious belief, and the relation between belief and science, are bound to come up. Some arise directly from the modern study of religion: How far can we account for religious ideas by saying that they are projections whose origins lie in ourselves and in human society? To what extent can we think of religion as being an area of experience, like music or morality, with its own principles and its own inner dynamic? What difference do our theories about religions and ideologies make to the way we are to see the future of human beliefs?

The Future of Belief

I want to explore the answers to these questions in light of the writers and theories we have already alluded to. My argument is itself a brief kind of speculation—some suggestions about ways we might look at religion and the secular worldviews. I shall do so by looking at the three points of the triangle that worldviews refer to: the cosmos, the self, and society.

First, the cosmos. We may draw a line between those who adopt a humanist view and those who, as in traditional religions, have a belief in some ultimate Being beyond the cosmos. For the so-called scientific humanist there is nothing to know which lies outside of this universe of ours. But for the traditional believer the cosmos wears another face; for the theist it is the creation of a good God; for the Buddhist it is the cycle of rebirth beyond which lie ultimate liberation and Emptiness; for the Taoist its inner unseen nature is the Way. We have already seen how, according to one form of modern existentialist philosophy (in the writings of Bultmann and Buber), we should see personal relations as lying outside the area of scientific inquiry. These relations, in their most authentic form, are the province of religion.

A similar view of different origins comes from the later writings of the philosopher Ludwig Wittgenstein and others influenced by him. In this view, religious language has its own inner logic, and the religious believer does not differ from others concerning facts about the world but rather brings his or her own set of pictures to bear in interpreting those facts. He or she sees the world as having been created by a God, for instance, or lives in light of the picture of the Second Coming. Such "seeing as" or "picturing" does not exist in the same dimension as science. It is an alternative way of seeing and experiencing the same cosmos that science tries to understand—though with very different motives and tools.

The existentialist and the Wittgensteinian approaches can be called "two-aspect," in the sense that scientific knowledge and religious perception see the same thing (the cosmos) under two aspects, as on the one hand open to scientific exploration and on the other hand as conveying religious meaning.

It seems to me that such a two-aspect theory provides a way for many scientifically educated people to begin to harmonize science and religion. But more has to be said, because the idea that we see the cosmos as this or that stresses content—the results of scientific inquiry or of religious faith—but it does not say anything about method. After all, science is not so much a set of results (although it produces many results) as a way of unlocking the secrets of the cosmos, a method by which we enter into dialogue with nature. This method is a matter of observation and measurement. But you cannot say the same of religion, which is not a way of observing, per se, although it does include a way in which a person lays himself open to experience.

Thus, if there is a method in religion, it is not the same as the so-called scientific method. It is rather a method of prayer, of contemplation, of exposing the self to the ultimate. One might say that religion opens one up to the numinous and to the mystical. If there is a method it is a kind of self-preparation for experience of the Beyond.

Religion in this view is a way of coming to experience (among other things) the cosmos. It is seeing the things in this world around us as having a special set of meanings. It is not so much trying to understand how they work, but rather seeing them in the light of eternity. There is here a likeness between religion and painting. The painting gives us new eyes to see sunflowers or canals or people or fruit. A painting does not theorize about these things; it sees them both in new ways and "as they are." The painter gives an immediate force to what he paints. And the person who has a religious view of things sees them as having a special, "immediate" force and meaning. The sun becomes a sign of God's power, and benevolence, and sometimes wrath; the morning mist gives a sense of immediacy and impermanence.

Religion, however, cannot be untouched by the unspoken thoughts of a scientific culture. Science is always revising itself. Today's theories may be scrapped tomorrow, and nature has many surprises in store for us. So there is an element in science that is *critical*—a point much emphasized in the writings of Karl Popper (b. 1902). Science advances through the criticism and testing of theories. Good theories are those that survive such criticism. In a modern society a degree of openness in which our theories can be fully criticized is essential if science and technology are to flourish. Such a society obviously cannot be an authoritarian one. So how can authoritarian *religion* blend with such an open and scientific culture?

If symbols of authority—the Pope, the Bible, the guru, the charismatic leader—persist in religion, it is probably because they are being seen increasingly as ways and means of discipline. They are themselves symbols and persons who help us in the pursuit of that opening up to God or ultimate freedom. Just as Buddhism, in its seeking for a glimpse of that enlightenment that suffused the Buddha's consciousness, has created the society of the Sangha, or monastic order, with its rules and rather strict discipline, so too other religions have used authority as a means toward a higher experience. But such authority is bound to be modified in the context of the open society. And increasingly, men and women who accept the discipline of an authority do so because they have chosen to do so. In a plural and open world, there is no compulsion to accept this or that. So in its own way religion is likely to become more and more "empirical"; that is, it is likely to be seen as testable in experience, a matter of "come and see."

Yet such openness creates its own backlashes. The freedom and ability to choose, which are characteristics of a plural society, often create their own problems. People often feel a need to go back to a purer authority—a kind of fundamentalism, a literalness, a faithful acceptance of what one is told. So, side by side in the emerging global culture with a new free and easy individual kind of religion, there is likely to be a whole array of backlashes, of often harsh reaffirmations of older moral, social, and doctrinal stances.

We can distinguish two main forms that the religious "vision" of the cosmos can take. One sees the cosmos as having "behind" it a personal Being. The other sees it as having "behind" or "within" it something eternal and yet indescribable—a Way, Emptiness, nir-vana. The one vision is nourished by devotion and the experience of the numinous, the other by the practice of self-control and the inner mystical experience.

The two visions sometimes blend, so that the Beyond is also "within" and the personal has an unspoken depth. This type of vision is important if we are trying to estimate how the religious understanding of the self may fare in the modern world. There remains in each human being a feeling that we find meaning both outwardly, in relation to the people we know and love and the things we do and possess, and inwardly, in relation to what lies in back of all our experiences. Each of us is a center of consciousness. We often feel that the world would not exist without our own individual consciousness. For aren't we the ones who somehow impose on the great flux out there the shapes, smells, sounds, and sensations that arise from our consciousness? The cosmos as we know it is the result of an interaction between what is mysteriously out there and what lies within. It is as if the atoms and molecules and particles whose swarms make up the world around us are nothing at all in themselves, until they spring into life when lit up by the multicolored light of our consciousness. One of the quests of the yogi and the mystic has been to search out that ego—the pure consciousness that lies in back of all our experiences—to find, as it were, the true essence of ourselves, and so the pure essence of the light that lights up the world.

The outer sense of the personal behind the cosmos and the inner quest for pure consciousness are both reflections of the fact that the universe has to be interpreted in the light of our existence. However small and insignificant this planet may be against the great face of the galaxy-sprinkled cosmos, it is nevertheless inhabited by conscious human beings. The materialist begins with matter and sees consciousness just as a special species of matter—matter in its most refined form. But we can look at things the other way around: Matter is seen in quite a new light when we see that out of it emerges consciousness. Why not see matter as oriented toward consciousness? And could it not be that there is a divine consciousness behind the material cosmos? These options of belief and interpretation remain open to us. And because the mystery of our self-consciousness remains great, religious traditions will still represent to us possible experiments in living.

Moreover, the patterns of religious experience will still continue to bubble up in the human soul, whatever their ultimate origins and whether or not they give us an insight into something Beyond.

From this point of view religious experience is likely to remain a thread in human culture and life. It will continue to breed for us its own special ways of seeing, and feeling about, the world. How to interpret it is another matter. It might even be that a kind of religious humanism could emerge in which the numinous character of the cosmos is recognized, not one showing that there is a God, but one offering a way of responding to the wonders of life. In this way religion would take its place alongside art and music as a form of response and creativity.

Such as "religions humanism" is already prefigured in the writing of Jung. His idea is that in the unconscious there are certain deep patterns of symbolism that are manifested in myth and art and that help to express and to solve problems of living—problems such as how to understand and face evil. Jung's theory suggests that traditional religion supplies ways of bringing about wholeness in our personal lives. Such a humanism is richer than the usual Western variety, which simply stresses the need to value and revere human beings without recourse to God. Jungian humanism, however, makes some use of the resources of religious myth. And here the comparative study of religion has a vital task to perform, for now there lie before us the myths of all the world that can be explored for their capacity to bring to the surface those symbols of male and female, of wholeness and disintegration, of good and evil, of creation and destruction—all the myths which have arisen in the human race's long experience of the mysterious give-and-take with a delightful but threatening cosmos.

So we can say that a variety of religious options and possibilities continues to open up, even in the more unified world of the global city.

As we have seen, myth is not just a matter of a symbolic way of looking at the world, it is a way of coming to an understanding of one's own identity. The modern counterpart of this is history: It is through the rediscovery of the past that we know who "we" are. We have been passing through, and still are passing through, a period in which the primary political force has been nationalism. Thus, the nation or ethnic group must make its own history and its own roots. But there are signs that broader forms of history are becoming more meaningful. For instance, black Africa is evolving its own consciousness of what it is to be African. This new sense of the African past is a guide to the special role blacks can play in the evolving culture of the globe: Africa can revitalize music and art and expressions of joy and responses to suffering. In the Pacific there are attempts to express the "Pacific way"—the style of living and culture characteristic of the South Pacific as a whole, in the light of a shared ancestry and history. Already there is a sense of the history and destiny of the West—that is, primarily Europe and North America—as creating a scientific and individualistic civilization.

Among these patterns, the great religious traditions will more and more ask themselves what the meaning of their past is in view of the present unification of the globe. There may still be dreams in some religions of becoming, so to say, the church for the whole globe, as Christianity did for the "known world" of the Roman Empire. But it seems more plausible that religions will function more as denominations and sometimes as sects. They will be denominations in the sense that they will live together with a certain mutual recognition, each perhaps feeling that it has the right slant on life, but not altogether excluding the visions and values of the other traditions. Each will strive to bear witness to its own true self, and to spread such light as it possesses, but without the real hope of becoming the exclusive faith of all the world. Because such a tolerant attitude is in some degree threatening to the authority and certainty of the past, the backlashes in each faith will take the form of a global sectarianism. The conservative and traditionalist response to pluralism is to reaffirm the exclusive rightness of one's tradition and one's revelation. This will involve a degree of inner withdrawal from the concerns of the wider world. It will involve a kind of isolationism. We can see this happening in areas of the Islamic and Christian worlds, among Hindu militants, and occasionally in the new religions of Japan.

All these various changes and responses are relevant to the way in which we may come to understand society—to understand one another. There is here a certain tug of war. In a new and often disturbing interaction between cultures and ideologies, it is natural for different groups to try to affirm their own special identities. Sometimes traditional religion will be an important ingredient—Buddhism as shaping Sinhalese identity, Orthodoxy as shaping Romanian identity, Zulu Zionism as giving new meaning to Zulu identity, and so on. But at the same time we are shaping a global society. How is the identity of that society to be understood? As the identity of the human race, no less. But this itself implies that we should see human history as a whole in a new light. Those who see it just as exhibiting the rhythms of the Marxist dialectic, or the unfolding guidance of Allah, may have to come to terms with a more plural approach. For if, as I have suggested, there is likely to be a denominational trend in the great religions, there is also likely to be what might be described as a "federalist" trend in world history. The global society will be looking back to a variety of histories—Russian, Chinese, American, African, Pacific, and so on. From the insights into and experiences of these various civilizations the tapestry of a new world civilization will be woven. Even if each tradition stays true to its own message, it will have to operate in a context of this federal world civilization.

Such a development will give the history of religions an interesting role to play in education. It is a role foreshadowed by Eliade, who suggests that the history of religions interprets for the modern world the world of archaic men. I would put it differently: In addition to trying to describe as accurately as possible, and with structured empathy, the meaning of past forms of religion, we may also wish to see what those forms still contain in the way of creative messages for our own global civilization. We thus have a modern form of the cult of ancestors. In traditional societies there is communication with the ancestral dead; now we, too, can achieve contact with Zarathustra, the Buddha, Christ, Maimonides, Ghazali, Mencius, and Marx through the medium of history.

Worldview analysis enables us to communicate not only with our spiritual ancestors but also with one another. In that goal we find the creative task of making ourselves mutually intelligible. Here too it may be possible to reflect upon the lessons offered by different cultures and belief-systems. I am not, of course, presupposing here that everything is good in other cultures or in our own. We need to be critical as well as appreciative. But by what criteria? That, of course, is the crucial question. At the very least we can agree that each culture has some distinctive contribution to make to our understanding of the world.

Moreover, the very "federalism" of the emerging global civilization and the study of religions and worldviews may themselves offer clues about how to evaluate the creative uses of the past.

First, it seems to me that the very process of establishing a federal approach to cultures implies an attempt to combine loyalty to one's tradition with respect, and so toleration, for the traditions of others. It is worth noting here that the candid exploration of religions and worldviews, now so vividly a part of the Western intellectual scene (not just through the study of religion but also through the human and social sciences), is not possible in monistic societies as I defined them earlier. The open exploration of diverse commitments and identities does not flourish in a closed society, where the distinction between party and the state, as in China or North Korea, or between religion and the state, as in Saudi Arabia or the Sudan, is not clearly and appropriately made. But an important part of empathy and tolerance is the capacity to understand some of the insecurities that can breed intolerance. A tolerant society should be able to withstand a fair amount of intolerant language and opinion; likewise, a tolerant globe can put up with a degree of intolerance. Only when there is a real and urgent threat to tolerance do the tolerant need to take action.

Second, a critical approach to religions and worldviews has to look to what the main point or objective of a system of belief is. We can evaluate Christianity by its capacity for love, and its commitment to live a spiritual life close to God. We can judge Buddhism by its insight and compassion. We can judge liberalism by its actual social reforms and efforts toward a better life for ordinary people. It will probably turn out that the various goals and central objectives of the differing faiths are not all that incompatible. Such compatibility already suggests ways of cooperation.

Third, because it seems that there are no proofs for or against the validity of any worldview, people should accept that different ways of life are, so to speak, different experiments in living. None can lay claim to an absoluteness. Such absoluteness is not available until the end of time when all perhaps will be revealed. (But even then the belief that there is an end to time is itself one of the things that may be disputed and argued about in that soft and hazy way that is demanded by the actual situation.)

But—it may be answered—many people believe in faith, and in one faith alone. Some take the Bible as absolute; others the Qur'ān; others the Vedas; others the Marxist tradition. People do, in fact, lay claim to an absoluteness, and it is not for me to look down on those of fervent commitment. But it must be said that the certitude of those who have such faith is not a public certitude. The faithful often think that what they see so clearly is obvious to others. It is not so. If it were, there would be no great divergences between worldviews. So while certitude must be respected, it is not something that rests on outer proof. It may be that the search for proofs is a snare that the religious and others would do well to avoid.

Fourth, the impulse to walk in others' moccasins already implies respect for others. Such respect is heightened, perhaps, by the thought that human beings have that consciousness that is the silent turning point of the whole world—or perhaps by the belief that they reflect something from the Beyond. But respect is not, of course, just a matter of understanding the others' point of view. Respect implies that one acknowledge the dignity of the other. So it seems to me that one test of a religion or worldview is the degree to which it is actually able to help those whose dignity is threatened by poverty or humiliation, by cruelty or callousness. Religion can never seal itself off from the cry of those who are in distress, and retain its integrity.

As a result of this test it may turn out that "true" religion is not to be identified with any tradition as a whole, but rather with individual movements and people within it. There are, after all, both callous Christianities and compassionate ones. This is another lesson we can draw from the study of worldviews: There are many more varieties than at first meet the eye; and our broad categories of "-isms" are often misleading, for they simplify a human world of great complexity. But maybe that is good. It is as though we see a hillside full of flowers, some yellow, some purple, some red, some white, some blue, and think that there are five sorts of flowers. But when we come among them we find each color covers a swarm of differing kinds of flowers, so many that the true classifications cross the boundaries of color; white and purple clover at first belonged apart, but upon a closer look are seen to be close sisters.

The kind of federalism I have been advocating may also be useful as a banner for the smaller cultures on our planet. I think we can safely say that the old world of the anthropologist is fading away very rapidly. Indian villages in the highlands of Guatemala, once a world of their own, now receive on cheap transistors the insistent messages of a global world, while guerrillas and government officials suck them into wider political struggles than they have ever known. Remote African nomadic tribes are now visited by experts in cattle raising and are beginning to tap the silent waves of the air. Those in remote New Guinea valleys are now asked to vote and to sell their pigs for market. Coral islands see the cruise ships and the frigates of great white powers circling like predators. There is hardly a tribe or small people left untouched by huge and accelerating waves of outside influence. The disturbance can be both entrancing and threatening. If small-scale societies embrace new religions, it may be one sign that they wish to cope with change by somehow reaffirming their own identity. And ultimately, although they need to live in a wider world, they need also to see their own place in it. This is hard to do; but it is a social and psychological project that breathes, perhaps quite unknowingly, the spirit of federalism, the federalism of the spirit that seems to be one major trend in a shrinking but divergent world.

There will be many surprises in the ferment. We are drawing to the end of an epoch in which older philosophies had great dynamism—the utilitarianism of the West, Marxisms, existentialism—and older religions still have great self-confidence. We are entering a new phase of human history, and in that phase the study of religions and analysis of worldviews have a great part to play.

These chapters have been an invitation to the field of religious study. Finally and briefly I shall suggest ways in which it is possible for you to travel further.

Postscript

Further Explorations
in Religion
and Worldview Analysis

Usually a book like this lists books for further reading, and indeed here I also make some suggestions. But it is worth remembering that books are only one means toward understanding the world. In the case of religions and worldviews it is useful, I think, to use the six dimensions—experiential, mythic, doctrinal, ethical, ritual, and social—as a kind of checklist, so that you can approach any religious movement or tradition in a reasonably rounded way. Once you look to those dimensions you will see very quickly that the world beyond books holds many other keys to understanding. For instance, if you are exploring the Roman Catholic tradition you will need most of all to get a feel for the Mass. One of the best ways, indeed an essential way, is to attend the Mass if you are not already familiar with it. You will then be a "participant observer." In that way you will be taking part in fieldwork, much as an anthropologist might in some culture that he or she seeks to understand.

If you are already familiar with the Mass, it is probably because you are a Roman Catholic or have been brought up in that tradition. There are pitfalls here. You may think you understand it better than you do. Familiarity may lead to the dulling of questions.

The person to whom the Mass is strange will sometimes have a fresher grasp of some of its outstanding features. Moreover, there is always more to learn about any tradition even if you know a lot about it already. For instance, the structure of the contemporary Mass has to be understood against the background of what happened at and after Vatican II. That again presupposes some idea of the period before, when the structure of the Mass was dictated by the tradition of the Council of Trent—in an era when the architecture and painting of churches tended to have a certain baroque style, rich and dark and heavily adorned. As for the other religious dimensions, you need to understand many things, such as what is distinctive about Catholic ethics; what the shape of Catholic doctrine is; the story of the Church as seen through Catholic eyes; the nature of Catholic mysticism and the particular style of the Catholic sense of the numinous; the shape of Catholic institutions; and above all, the Papacy. In addition you have to realize that although Catholicism is worldwide it exists in many varieties. The darker and more austere forms of Irish Catholicism differ from the more exuberant and carefree Italian Catholicism, and both differ from the activist Catholicism of the United States. Happily, ours is an age when travel is easy. If you have eyes to see there is much to find out about forms of faith in foreign lands.

It is easy, if you live in Madison, Wisconsin, or in Edinburgh, Scotland, to do your "fieldwork" next door, by going around to the nearest Presbyterian or Catholic Church. It might seem more difficult to do fieldwork on, say, Buddhism. But still, the same six-dimensional checklist can be used, and although the fuller fieldwork—seeing Buddhism in some of its typical Eastern environments—may be something that has to be postponed until you can travel, there are in our Western societies many minorities from Eastern cultures. There are also many people who have joined Eastern religions. You do not, after all, have to go to India to see Buddhist meditation in action. It is true that a religion outside its original cultural context will have changed. Some who know Buddhism from New York become disappointed in Sri Lanka, just as Christians from Nigeria are often disappointed with the faith they find (or do not find) in England, whence came the missionaries.

But if travel in the flesh is not always possible, you can travel in the mind. Not only can books take you richly into other minds, but there are many films which can give an insight into other faiths. For example, the BBC television series *The Long Search* is shown widely from time to time in the United States, Britain, and elsewhere. Other films such as Renoir's *The River* give a feel of other cultures and other realms.

In the formal study of religion, we often underestimate the insights that literature can provide. For example, E. M. Forster's *A Passage to India* gives a marvelous picture of some of the religious and cultural divergences in British India. There are, of course, many other major literary works of great religious depth, from Aeschylus and Shakespeare to Sartre and Solzhenitsyn.

Literature is, in part, just a portrayal of people, yet people seen through the lens of art. One can also, of course, see religions and worldviews through the eyes of people themselves. I earlier put great emphasis on structured empathy. This "entering into" other people's thought- and feeling-worlds is essential to the central descriptive task in the study of religion. But a major part of this "entering in" can be achieved by talking with people. What does the Christian faith mean to this person or another? What does Buddhism mean? Entering into a dialogue with someone is an important ingredient of further understanding. But we need to know how to ask and to frame the right questions.

This is one of the jobs of the teacher of religious studies: to help people to frame the right questions. A good introductory book in the field of religion and worldview analysis can give people that initial understanding that steers them away from foolish and blinding questions. It is not much good charging into the mind of a Buddhist with such a question as "Do you believe in God?", for, as we have seen, the worldview of Buddhism is completely different from the worldviews of the ancient Near East and the modern West (the worldviews that helped you frame that question).

Part of the problem of cultural and religious diversity is language. The person who wishes to explore the New Testament ought to realize that it was initially written in Greek, and that some of the translations we use are questionable. Thus *agapē* is translated as "charity" or as "love," words that in modern English usage have a different flavor from the Greek (the one veering toward alms-giving, and the other toward sex and romance). It is not possible for you to learn a whole language, perhaps, although it is surprising how many people manage to get caught up with the spell of such languages as Hebrew, Sanskrit, Pali, or Greek. But it is good to be aware of the problem, and often possible to learn at least some of the key ideas and the key features of a language. For instance, knowing about the way vowels were treated in writing Hebrew helps us to understand why there are often ambiguities of meaning in the original, and the fact that Chinese is monosyllabic, and not given to abstract nouns, tells us why there is a certain style of concreteness about classical Chinese texts. The myriad translations of the *Tao Te Ching*, the classic of Tao, become understandable when we notice the epigrammatic and laconic nature of much Chinese poetry. So even if we do not learn a language we can learn something about languages.

In talking of structured empathy I have in effect sketched a mode of travel into other minds, but usually we think of this in terms of my traveling here and now into the minds of others here and now. Religious traditions and secular worldviews require some time travel, however. The world of Paul is not our world, nor is the world of Karl Marx. We need imagination to feel what the Roman Empire and Palestine were like in the days of Paul, or what European capitalism and London life were like in the days of Marx. So part of our inquiry into worldviews must be historical. Here it is useful to read not just a history of religions, such as my own *The Religious Experience of Mankind* or Trevor Ling's *History of Religions East and West*. It is also important to read some wider account of the relevant culture: a history of the Roman Empire or of ancient India or of China.

The judicious use of encyclopedias is often useful, especially the so-called Macropedia section of the *Encyclopedia Britannica*. This has many excellent articles on the great religions and the religions of Africa and elsewhere. (It is rather weak, from our point of view as explorers of religion and culture, in its country-by-country accounts. Thus, if you look up a country such as Romania, you'll find little on the spiritual and intellectual side of Romanian history and culture, but more on the religious traditions as a whole.) The *Encyclopedia of Philosophy* contains a great deal on religious doctrines.

It is also a good idea, in developing a feel for religions and worldviews, to think about symbolism. This can often be done in the environment around us.

Symbols help to bring us to an understanding of the rituals of the social context in which we find ourselves such as the whole body of lore that centers around the meal. Thinking about the rituals attached to eating will help us understand communion, fasting, and other sacred approaches to food and drink.

The symbols of everyday life are also a bridge to understanding the visual language of sculpture and painting. Sit before a fine Buddha statue from India in one of our major galleries, or look at its photo in a fine art book, and ask yourself what messages it conveys. First of all you can do so without reference to the conventional parts of the iconography, like the arrangement of fingers and hands, which constitute a separate language which you need later to learn. You can start by thinking about the *spirit* of the sculpture. What does it communicate? Likewise with the Crucifix or an icon of the Virgin Mary. Or go into a church or temple and think about the meaning of its space. What do Gothic arches mean? What does the shape of a Buddhist temple complex convey?

There is a great deal in which we can immerse ourselves if we are going forward in the everyday exploration of religious and other values. But what (you might say) about inward practice? What about prayer? What about meditation? I think it is important to have at least a preliminary experience of the spiritual life. I do not mean by this that we necessarily should get converted, or be "born again" (but maybe you already are). I mean that because prayer and meditation have meant and continue to mean so much to so many, it is important for us to have an inkling of what it is like, if we do not have this knowledge already. Even if we have been brought up to say the Lord's Prayer or to go to synagogue, it does not follow that we know what the self-training of the mystic is like or what the sense of the presence of God is. Why not try to imagine what the religious life is like? Collections of mystical and devotional writings can tell you a lot. And why not try meditation, for that matter? Why not stay in a monastery? Even if you do not believe in God, why not act *as if* the world around us is continually speaking messages to us from the Creator?

None of this will mean that you will brainwash yourself some-how into adopting beliefs you do not truly hold. For religious experience needs to be interpreted, and it is you who will be supplying that framework. Perhaps inevitably you will be drawn into some reflections about the truth of religion and the truth of secular world-views (the truths are two sides of the same coin).

In order to do this, it is important to get some orientation in the philosophy of religion; there are a number of good modern writings that arise out of the debate about whether all knowledge has to be empirical—a matter of seeing, hearing, smelling. This debate is, in effect, the debate about scientific humanism: Is it necessary for all knowledge ultimately to be scientific (that is, knowledge based upon seeing, hearing, and so on, but expressed through mathematics and theories about what patterns lie behind what we see)?

It is also wise to ponder some of the best doctrinal writings of the modern age—ones that take Christian or Buddhist or whatever doctrine seriously and try to present them systematically. How does a person who has thought about his or her tradition come to give it meaningful shape in today's world?

It is wise always to see religion interacting with the other forces in our world. We need to see it in interplay with feminism, a powerful contemporary current, and with economic changes, including the increasing power and integration of transnational corporations. We need to see it in relation to the teeming politics of new and old nationalisms, especially where these have part of their basis in religions. We should see religion in relation to the poverty in our world—a great engine of faith, whether spiritual or secular, is hope. Hope is something the oppressed need to hear about—all of us need to hear about it, of course, but above all those who are losing out in this beautiful world.

A sensitive understanding of worldviews is a marvelous preparation for life in our world, and is a substantial ingredient in proper reflection on the nature and direction of our societies. The desire to explore the field further, to voyage both inwardly and outwardly through the symbols, experiences, and thought of human beings is not a luxury. It is an exciting quest and a noble part of our self-education. Voyage onward!

Further Reading

Some useful general introductions to the history of religions are:

Ian Harris et al., eds. *Contemporary Religions: A World Guide.* London: Longman, 1992.

Ninian Smart. *The Religious Experience*, 4th ed. New York: Macmillan, 1991.

——— *The World's Religions*. Englewood Cliffs, N.J.: Prentice Hall, 1989.

R. C. Zaehner, ed. *The Concise Encyclopaedia of Living Faiths.* Boston: Beacon, 1969.

Also helpful are the articles on religions and philosophy in *Encyclopedia Britannica*, Macropedia Section, especially the 1974 ed.; and **Mircea Eliade**, ed. *Encyclopedia of Religion*, 16 vols., New York: Macmillan, 1986.

On the history of the field and some of the major contributions:

Michael Banton, ed. *Anthropological Approaches to the Study of Religion.* New York: Methuen, 1968.

Rudolf Bultmann. *Jesus Christ and Mythology.* New York: Charles Scribner's Sons, 1958.

Mary Douglas. *Purity and Danger.* Boston: Routledge and Kegan Paul, 1978.

Émile Durkheim. *The Elementary Forms of the Religious Life*. Winchester, Mass.: Allen Unwin, 1976.

Murray Edelman. *The Symbolic Uses of Politics*. Champaign: University of Illinois Press, 1967.

Mircea Eliade. *The Quest*. Chicago: University of Chicago Press, 1975.

E. Evans-Pritchard. *Theories of Primitive Religion*. New York: Oxford University Press, 1968.

Sigmund Freud. *The Future of an Illusion*. New York: Norton, 1976.

John Hick. *The Philosophy of Religion*. Englewood Cliffs, N.J.: Prentice Hall, 1973.

William James. *The Varieties of Religious Experience*. New York: Macmillan, 1961.

C. G. Jung. *Symbols of Transformation*, 5 vols. Princeton, N.J.: Princeton University Press, 1976.

Hans Küng. *Does God Exist?* New York: Doubleday, 1980.

Claude Lévi-Strauss. *The Savage Mind*. Chicago: University of Chicago Press, 1966.

Trevor Ling. *Karl Marx and Religion*. Totowa, N.J.: Barnes and Noble Books, 1980.

W. J. M. Mackenzie. *Political Identity*. New York: St. Martin's, 1978.

John Macquarrie. *Twentieth Century Religious Thought*, revised ed. New York: Charles Scribner's Sons, 1981.

David Martin. *A General Theory of Secularization*. New York: Harper & Row, 1979.

Albert Moore. *Introduction to Religious Iconography*. Philadelphia, Pa.: Fortress, 1977.

Rudolf Otto. *The Idea of the Holy*. New York: Oxford University Press, 1958.

John Passmore. *A Hundred Years of Philosophy*. New York: Penguin, 1978.

David Roberts. *Existentialism and Religious Belief*. New York: Oxford University Press, 1959.

Eric J. Sharpe. *Comparative Religion—A History*. New York: Charles Scribner's Sons, 1975.

Ninian Smart. *Philosophers and Religious Truth*. New York: Macmillan, 1970.

———. *The Concept of Worship*. London: Macmillan, 1973.

———. *Beyond Ideology: Religion and the Future of Western Civilization*. New York: Harper and Row, 1981.

Wilfred Cantwell Smith *The Meaning and End of Religion*. New York: Harper & Row, 1978.

Frits Staal. *Exploring Mysticism*. Berkeley: University of California Press, 1975.

W. T. Stace. *Religion and the Modern Mind*. New York: Lippincott, 1960.

Ernst Troeltsch. *The Absoluteness of Christianity and the History of Religions*. Atlanta, Ga.: John Knox, 1971.

Victor Turner. *The Ritual Process*. Ithaca, N.Y.: Cornell University Press, 1977.

Gerardus van der Leeuw. *Religion in Essence and Manifestation*. Magnolia, Mass.: Peter Smith, 1967.

Arnold Van Gennep. *The Rites of Passage*. Chicago: University of Chicago Press, 1960.

Jacques Waardenburg. *Classical Approaches to the Study of Religion*, vols. 1 and 2. Hawthorne, N.Y.: Mouton, 1974

Joachim Wach. *The Comparative Study of Religions*. New York: Columbia University Press, l958.

Max Weber. *The Protestant Ethic and the Spirit of Capitalism*. New York: Charles Scribner's Sons, 1977.

Bryan Wilson. *Magic and the Millennium*. Brooklyn Heights, N.Y.: Beekman Publishers, 1978.

J.M. Yinger. *The Scientific Study of Religion*. New York: Macmillan, 1961.

Index